Praise for *Gomorrah Was Religious Too*

The religious church has become "a stockroom for the crumbs which fall from the world's table, rather than a storehouse for the bread of life." Commitment, religion's highest virtue, is only a substitute for true Christian love. But the Christian who ignores the imperatives of God's law, in the name of love, is a "love-only legalist" in his own right. These are only a few of the pithy insights Chris Surber offers in *Gomorrah Was Religious Too*. Be prepared to find some of your cherished opinions challenged by this author, whose passion for renewal in the church erupts on every page.

Richard C. Leonard
Laudemont Ministries - Laudemont Press
Biblical Theology, Worship Studies and Christian Fiction

This book is a wonderful tribute to Leonard Ravenhill, carrying the same burden for revival that much of his work focused on. Its cadence and literary beauty captivates the heart while its substance captivates the mind. This book may be the catalyst for revival that the Church so desperately needs. I pray that all who read it would catch the spark that drives the author; and that Christ would fan those sparks into a great flame of revival in His Church.

Lawrence E. Bray Th.D.
President, The North American Reformed Seminary

Chris Surber is a prophetic voice issuing an urgent and passionate wake-up call to the Church. Like the late Leonard Ravenhill, Surber's clear message drives a stake into the heart of religion masquerading as true faith, drawing adherents but never satisfying God's heart—or man's need—for the life-giving walk of a true disciple. Insightful, penetrating, and prayer provoking.

Dr. Harvey R. Brown, Jr.
President, Impact Ministries

If you are looking for avenues for appeasement or accommodation between contemporary Christian "religionists" and what is revealed in the Scriptures, then Gomorrah was Religious Too most certainly will disappoint. If, however, you are seeking the clear teachings and practices of what God desires from those who claim to be followers of His Son, you will be confronted, challenged and, through God's grace, comforted through Chris Surber's powerful prose: "Practitioners of powerless religion are like men drinking from empty cups...."

Karl Fivek, Ed.D.
Peru, Illinois

If Christians are the salt and light of the world, then why is the world still such a tasteless and dark place? Perhaps it is because the church, the body of Christ, has obsessed itself with "religious rules and practices," while the world needs the "reckless love" demonstrated on the cross. Chris Surber's indictment of modern Christian religion compels those who have received God's abundant grace to smash the idol of religion and replace it with the transformative grace of Jesus, rooted in an abject acknowledgement of our own sinfulness and God's call for repentance. Without that foundation, churches have become impotent tools, and Satan's work is half done.

Res Spears
Editor, Suffolk News-Herald
Suffolk Living Magazine
Suffolk, VA

Gomorrah Was Religious Too

by

Chris Surber

Energion Publications
P. O. Box 841
Gonzalez, FL 32560

2012

Cover Picture: © Federico Donatini | Dreamstime.com

ISBN10: 1-938434-04-8
ISBN13: 978-1-938434-04-4
Library of Congress Control Number: 2012940746

Energion Publications
P. O. Box 841
Gonzalez, FL 32560

(850) 525-3916
energionpubs.com

For my wife Christina
with whom I share the journey of faith.

Contents

AUTHOR NOTE

My desire to pen this book grew out of reading the works of the late author and evangelist, Dr. Leonard Ravenhill. In fact, the title of this book, *"Gomorrah Was Religious Too,"* is a tip of the hat to Ravenhill's work, *Sodom Had No Bible.* In our day, as in the not so distant past days of Leonard Ravenhill, revival tarries because we tarry. God yet desires to purify His Church with the winds of revival in the power of the Holy Spirit to free His people from the pauper's rags of religion to the princely robes of our adoption in Jesus Christ.

I wrote this book for all those who desire to follow after Christ sincerely, no pretense, no dishonesty, no self deception, and no duplicity. I wrote this book for me. I stumbled quite by accident onto Leonard Ravenhill's writing. In fact, I was online doing some research for a sermon and my heart almost jumped out of my chest when I read the title of his book, *Sodom Had no Bible.* I said out loud, late at night in my study, "You got that right! Neither do we!" Time and again while reading Ravenhill, I am struck by the power of his words brought about by his reliance on God's Word.

His words, etched in paper with quill and ink, speak to me on a deep level because I am, as I suspect he was, weary of *religion* and deeply desirous of the revelation of God to spark revival in the Church. After less than a decade in the pastoral ministry, I have experienced, witnessed, or seen firsthand the spiritual, emotional, familial, social, and even financial havoc that religion is wreaking on the revolution that Jesus inaugurated in His own blood. In the name of the Master of Mercy, self-righteousness and judgment reigns. In the name of the Prince of Peace, local churches and the reputation of Christ is demolished by hateful conflict.

I wrote this book for me because in its pages are recorded my longings for what the Church can be; what every local gathering of followers and seekers of Jesus Christ should be. I cannot move forward without acknowledging my indebtedness to the thought and prose of Leonard Ravenhill. They were the driving force behind the collection of sermons which provides the seminal thoughts for this book. As with Ravenhill's writing, the goal of this book is not rebuke, but encouragement to rebuild. These are not words of condemnation for religious idolatry, but encouragement to escape from the trap of religion.

This book has been penned from a burning desire to see the Church cast out religion and pick up the Cross. The writing of Ravenhill has greatly fueled my imagination concerning what the Church can be if she will open her Bible in honesty, pray with penitent sincerity, strap on her sandals, pick up her walking stick, and follow after Jesus, rather than to sit comfortably in her pews, happily trading in the revelation of Jesus for the religion of man.

Introduction

The world perishes while we waste our spiritual lives engaged in meaningless religion. The Church is fed a steady stream of lies we *want* rather than the truth that we *need*. As a result, our spiritual senses are dull. We greatly prefer the standard fare of the modern church in our land. Man-centered, ego-boosting sermons, spiritual get-rich-quick schemes, and vague rhetoric has largely replaced straightforward Bible preaching, teaching, and conviction in the hearts of Jesus followers. Religion fails us at every turn. We are neither happy nor satisfied. We offer a poor witness to the world around us.

We most often display a disharmonious false religious piety to the world and then rather than understanding that it is our contentious spirits which drives them only further from the Church, we judge them for their sin. *Gomorrah Was Religious Too* is an appropriate title for this book, though it must be made clear at the outset that this is not a book full of tirades against modern culture. I have little interest in berating those who do not know Jesus for their lack of Christ-likeness. How deep is the hypocrisy so many in our day who belittle the culture for its lack of love for God when the Church itself is so desperately in want for a love affair with the Most High.

We who know Jesus should fall on our faces in repentance for the mockery of His message that we portray in our religious devotion, which is most often utterly devoid of Christ-like love for sinners and fervor for the glory of God. The puritan preacher of old, Thomas Manton, once wrote that "Divisions in the church al-

1

ways breed atheism in the world."[1] Surely every believer recognizes the inherent truth in that statement. However, in recognizing that truth are we willing to do what it takes to live harmoniously? Are we even capable of doing what it takes? Has our religious enterprise even given us the spiritual tools necessary for the task at hand?

These are the kinds of questions we will explore together in the following pages. Perhaps together we can – *at the very least* – learn to recognize the difference between dead religion and the living breathing life of Jesus when His life is infused into a community of believers and present in individual hearts. If we can learn to recognize it perhaps we will develop an appetite for it, a longing that will lead to desperation on our part to create it, by God's grace working in us.

I have lived several years in cold northern climates but I grew up in temperately moderate North Central California. Consequently, I am amazed at the difference between the appearance of snowy northern places in winter and spring. In the height of winter in Northern Michigan, where my family lived briefly, snow covers everything. Old buildings, whose edifice cries out for demolition, appear to be a part of a magical scene when they are covered by a foot or more of snow that drapes over the edge of rooftops from which dangle long mystical ice crystals through which the sunlight dances and plays. The wretchedly ugly potholes of old city streets are filled and disappear to the eye as powdery snow-fluff packs them in.

Then comes springtime with its rays of hot sun and the snow vanishes. Muck and mud are left in its place. The beauty departs and what was there all along but covered with placid snow becomes visible again. Similarly, we can cover our sin, our brokenness, our judgmental attitudes, our vices, and our rebellion to God with religion in the idolatrous winter of our life, but spring will inevitably come. Religion masks our desperate need for God. It does noth-

---

1   Thomas Manton, *The Complete Works of Thomas Manton*, (London: James Nisbet & Company, 1871), 69.

ing to bring His hope and healing into the lives of our faith communities, nor does it bring healing into our broken lives.

I have never eaten a plastic decorative apple and I don't intend to do so. Surely you would agree with me that to eat a piece of plastic fruit from a holiday decoration would be pure madness. Why is it not considered madness to do the same with our worship of the God who saves us from sin and its consequences? Why are so many believers content with going through the motions of religious activity, religious entertainment, or the mere act of keeping our churches "going," rather than wading in the deep waters of knowing God and making Him known?

It is not an exaggeration for this pastor to say that the single biggest obstacle to authentic connectedness to God in Jesus Christ is more often than not the religious structures, idolatry, divisions, judgment, and false piety of religious people and the structures that they build and maintain in the name of Jesus. That may be difficult to read. Good. I would never return to a doctor who could plainly see that my arm was disease ridden and on the verge of rotting right off of my body and, for the sake of not damaging my frail emotional sensibilities, patted me on the back and sent me on my way.

Nor would I be guilty of one of the gravest sins being committed week in and week out in pulpits throughout our land. People-pleasing-grinning-cowardly pulpiteers of every sort lovingly pat on the back spiritually dying men and women on their way to eternity without Christ for the sake of not offending their audiences, largely in the hopes that those audiences will continue to grow. In such a manner *we* are terrible successes at filling pews and at the same time crowding the streets of Hell. It is not my intention or goal to belittle or berate the Body of Christ. Just as a loving mother or father steers their child back to the center of the sidewalk to avoid the danger of the road as they ride their bicycle, it is my goal to challenge and encourage the Church to come back to the center of our faith in order to avoid the onslaught of false religion.

It is the interplay between man's religion and God's revelation that we will discuss in what follows. It is to the aim of uncovering,

3

discovering, and applying what we discover that we will move. False religion to the exclusion of authenticity in following Christ is vile in the sight of God. "'Come now, let us reason together,' says the LORD. 'Though your sins are like scarlet, they shall be as white as snow; though they are red as crimson, they shall be like wool'" (Isaiah 1:18). There is hope for the body of Christ! There is an endless reservoir of superabundant grace awaiting all who cry out to Him in sincerity.

The ink for the quill which penned these words was drawn from the broken places in the heart of a pastor who aches for a return to the revelation of Jesus alone and the destruction of the false religion which plagues the world in His name.

1

Detestable Incense, Meaningless Offerings

> Hear the word of the LORD, you rulers of Sodom; listen to the law of our God, you people of Gomorrah! "The multitude of your sacrifices – what are they to me?" says the LORD. "I have more than enough of burnt offerings, of rams and the fat of fattened animals; I have no pleasure in the blood of bulls and lambs and goats. When you come to appear before me, who has asked this of you, this trampling of my courts? Stop bringing meaningless offerings! Your incense is detestable to me." – Isaiah 1:10-13

It is simply not possible to have any valid concept of true religion until we understand the nature of sin. God has especially revealed Himself to mankind through the words of the prophets, the Bible, and ultimately Jesus Christ. Sinners everywhere have always had concepts about God and religious structures but these have not brought them any closer to God. The revelation of God in Jesus Christ represents the obliteration of religion, not the institution, alteration, or continuation of it. Jesus brings an entirely new set of paradigms into our understanding of religion, God, and self.

We don't need religion. We need an entirely new way of relating to God because our sin separates us from God. That's right at the heart of the problem though. We don't realize how desperate our situation is and as a result we live under the misguided impression that we have the power to do something about it. Religion can be many things and in the contents of this book we will flesh out some of the ways false religion is destroying the movement that Jesus inaugurated at His coming. Chief among them is approaching our religious activity with a heart that is divorced from a clear understanding of the nature of sin.

Our sin is detestable in the sight of God. That is precisely because it robs Him of His glory in us. God's holiness and glory are central in this universe, not our comfort and well being, not our satisfaction and happiness. Our religious efforts, when they are devoid of the genuine articles of faith are detestable. Our religious efforts are meaningless unless and to the extent that they grow out of dependence upon Him rather than an attempt to garner His favor. In other words, incense and offerings—religion—do not contain any inherent value. They are only as valuable as they are shells which contain *repentance* and faith.

Let us be clear at the outset. You and I are rebels of the highest degree in the economy of God's creation. We are blasphemers and slanderers because of our careless words, destroyers of the image of God in one another because of our judgmental hearts, murderers because of our anger. Worse yet, we are idolaters because we have remade God in our own image and *begged* for preaching and teaching that satisfies our egos rather than glorifies God.

We don't seek revival in our day; we seek to have our own religious idolatrous preferences affirmed by forceful but empty preaching, new buildings, new faces but not necessarily new converts on Sunday morning, and the appearance of worldly success. We do church in a manner that is consistent with the way business seeks growth. Please the customer and don't upset the employees. What is modeled in fellowships all across our land in this day is by and large a concept of following Jesus that is completely at war with the teachings and example of Jesus.

We cheapen the Gospel and minimize the value and purpose of the local fellowship of believers. Let us be clear. Let us be courageous enough to take an honest appraisal of the church landscape of which we are a part. We don't have to look to Adam to find our need for a savior. Idolatry and false worship abounds today. The late Leonard Ravenhill, a man whose writing has had great influence over this writer and on the penning of these chapters, wrote:

> Almost every Bible conference majors on today's Church being like the Ephesian Church. We are told that, despite our sin and carnality, we are seated with Him. Alas, what a lie! We are Ephesians all right; but, as the Ephesian Church in the Revelation, we have "left our first love!" We appease sin – but do not oppose it. To such a cold, carnal, critical, care-cowed Church, this lax, loose, lustful, licentious age will never capitulate. Let us stop looking for scapegoats. The fault in declining morality is not radio or television. The whole blame for the present international degeneration and corruption lies at the door of the Church! It is no longer a thorn in the side of the world. Yet, it has not been in times of popularity but of adversity that the true Church has always triumphed.[2]

It wasn't altogether different in the days of the prophet Isaiah. In his day, Israel was a rebellious and sinful nation, though they were not without their *religion*. Here the prophet even draws a parallel with Sodom and Gomorrah. In Isaiah 1:4 the prophet laments the state of His people:

> "Ah, sinful nation, a people loaded with guilt, a brood of evildoers, children given to corruption! They have forsaken the LORD; they have spurned the Holy One of Israel and turned their backs on him."

This is exactly the opposite of that for which Israel had been created by God. In Deuteronomy 7:6 it is said of Israel:

> For you are a people holy to the LORD your God. The LORD your God has chosen you out of all

---

2   Leonard Ravenhill, *Why Revival Tarries* (Minneapolis, Minnesota: Bethany House Publishers, 1986), 56.

the peoples on the face of the earth to be his people, his treasured possession.

The nation of Israel was chosen by God as an instrument through whom God would bring the Messiah. Just as the young girl Mary was the direct instrument of delivering the Messiah into this world, Israel acted as the broader channel through whom the revelation of God would descend. Israel's national identity as God's chosen people and their religion as direct worship of the one true and living God was always intended as a channel of blessing to all of the nations and all of the people of the earth.

In Genesis 12:1-3 it is exactly this that the Lord is declaring to Abram (later Abraham) when He called him to leave his homeland and trust God in faith:

> The LORD had said to Abram, "Leave your country, your people and your father's household and go to the land I will show you. I will make you into a great nation and I will bless you; I will make your name great, and you will be a blessing. I will bless those who bless you, and whoever curses you I will curse; and all peoples on earth will be blessed through you."

Through Israel, God proclaims the good news of salvation in Jesus Christ. Israel was the instrument of God's *revelation*, but time and again they got stuck in *religion*. God's plan for Israel throughout their history was to bring healing and redemption through the direct revelation of Jesus to the nations – not simply the foundation of modern Christian religion. Here in chapter one of Isaiah, the Israelites are a reproach to God. Rather than putting future redemption on display through their righteous living and adoration of God, they only practice religion in the same inward manner of the pagans who worship a multitude of false gods all around them.

Rather than pointing the way to the coming Messiah through righteousness, obedience, inward commitment to God, and obedience to His will, they desecrate the worship of God with their *religion*. Imagine, God is actually declaring in Isaiah chapter 1 that the very activity that is supposed to be directed to God in an effort to honor Him is detestable! In the strongest possible terms God denounces the religious activity of His chosen people because their hearts are not right before Him. God is infinitely more concerned with a heart that receives His revelation of Himself in humility and repentance than He is with a false piety put on display outwardly. The former honors God as the source of life while the latter puffs up self because it is rooted in human pride.

Right at the heart of their sinfulness was their false religion. Their sin was not that they fulfilled their religious obligations and made sacrifices before the Lord. God had given them instructions to do so. Their sin was the manner in which they performed their religious ceremonies. The Lord, through the prophet, declares to them: "Your hands are full of blood; wash and make yourselves clean. Take your evil deeds out of my sight! Stop doing wrong, learn to do right! Seek justice, encourage the oppressed. Defend the cause of the fatherless, plead the case of the widow" (Isaiah 1:15-17).

Their unclean hands were the result of their wrong hearts. Their religion had taken the place of adoration of the God who reveals Himself. Their sin was that of presumption; presuming God to be at the beck and call of those who perform religious activity, rather than the source of life and object of adoration. They sought to gain the favor of God by their religion, but they neglected the weightier things that gives religion meaning; seeking justice, encouraging the oppressed, the fatherless, the widows.

They made sacrifices and recited many prayers, but they forgot the message of God. There is no return to God's favor without amendment of life. Of course we have the great advantage of the fullness of God's revelation in the New Testament and in the life of Christ. In Luke 15:7 Jesus says, "I tell you that in the same way there will be more rejoicing in heaven over one sinner who repents than over ninety-nine righteous persons who do not need to repent."

Repentance is a matter of the heart. True repentance always manifests in the realm of actions but that is only evidence of its origin from within the heart. Repentance that begins with action is often little more than a mimic of the real thing. An outward expression of religion which does not proceed from a heart that is genuinely broken over sin is detested by God. When we exercise religion without exercising faith, we make God our servant. We put *Him* in *our* debt.

In the ancient pagan world animal and grain sacrifices, among other types of sacrifices, were seen as a way of gaining favor with the gods. This was not connected to a Judaic form of worship and sacrifice as a symbol of obedience. It was literally seen as a way of gaining favor with the gods because humans were providing the gods with a service that they could not or preferred not to do for themselves. It was actually seen as providing a meal for them.

> In fact, origin myths in Egypt and Mesopotamia portrayed humans as having been created as "servants or cattle of the gods. Specifically, they were to provide food for the gods, relieving them of having to do so." Such notions are absolutely foreign to true worship. Sacrifices in the Old Testament system were intended only as symbols of internal sacrifice to God and of the coming of Christ, who was the perfect sacrifice, a lamb without defect or blemish (I Peter 1:19).[3]

The sacrifice finds it ultimate expression in Jesus Christ who became our sacrifice to free us from sin through His blood. The sacrifice in the Old Testament and the sacrifice in the New Testament that God desires is the sacrifice of praise and obedience to Him. God, desiring to express His glory in us, uses our religion only as a vehicle, through which we make a commitment, through faith, to obedience to Him. He calls us, He reveals Himself to us, and then religion is used to bring the community of believers together in order to celebrate Him *alone*.

The problem comes in when we make our religious activity a means unto itself, a vehicle for displaying our goodness, or we de-

---

3   Baker, David W, Zondervan *Illustrated Bible Backgrounds Commentary*, ed. John H. Walton (Grand Rapids, Michigan: Zondervan, 2009), 11.

velop a club mentality. When we see the local assembly as a collection of righteous people in a building rather than a movement of forgiven sinners reaching up to God in thanksgiving and out to the world in hope, we pervert the purpose of the Church and we cheapen the Gospel. The Lord does not need us to make a dwelling for Him or to provide any material or spiritual sustenance for Him. He didn't create us because He was lonely. Nor did He create us because He had a need that only we could meet for Him.

God has existed throughout all of eternity in a triune mystery of perfect love and union within Himself. He chose to express that unity and love in creation. We are His creation and He needs nothing from us. The Israelites had fused pagan ideas with their worship. They were heavily committed to many prayers and many offerings that were done in the right pattern of worship, but the Bible makes it clear that their hearts were far from God. It is entirely possible to look good in the eyes of religious men, but make of our religion an idol which is detestable in the sight of God.

Many Church goers, who are not necessarily by definition Jesus followers, live in what can only be described as an overly romantic fog of religious apathy. They love to be patted on the back by smiling preachers who sacrifice truth for the sake of being nonoffensive with the Gospel. They are content to listen to the organ and chatter about the history of stained glassed windows and church edifices rather than to bend the knee of their heart to the lover of their souls. It has been well said that we are living in an age when our enemy Satan has little to fear from the Church because its effect is sorely diluted from having been inoculated with a mild case of Christianity so as to rob it of its zeal and puff it up with pride.

The Church must take careful measure of herself. She has slipped down the very same hill of idolatry and vanity as did those ancient Israelites to whom Isaiah spoke. Writing in *Christianity Today*, Katie Wiebe says:

> Whenever I attend yet another church spectator
> event, I am reminded of Tozer's disdain and despair

for "that strange thing—the program," for "conventional religious chatter," for our wholesale "pursuit of happiness, rather than holiness," for our bondage to the conscience of people rather than bondage to God.[4]

The early Church was characterized by suffering, persecution, a commitment to true godly wisdom, and yes, oh yes, God's care and provision through it all. When did phrases like "He's an entertaining public speaker" or "I go to that Church because they have the loveliest music" replace the desire and need of followers of Jesus to be nourished by the Word of God, grow in the power of the Holy Spirit, and to walk in unity as the people of God? The Church has, to a large extent, lost its prophetic voice because we have replaced a focus on *revelation* – what we need from God – with a focus on *religion* – what we *think* God needs from us. The way to get our prophetic voice back is to repent of our religion and imitate Christ.

What man or woman of God will heed such an encouragement in our day? Where are the people of God who so strongly desire to know God and His life working in them that they will apply this message?

The Church has become a counterfeit image of itself. More sadly, this is because it has mirrored the world rather than Christ. This world and our churches are equally filled with disingenuous forms of worship. Rather than worshiping the one who created us in the first place and recreates us in Christ, we focus on matters that please us rather than pleasing God.

The Church has become a stockroom for the crumbs which fall from the world's table, rather than a storehouse for the bread of life. Division, greed, divorce, anger, violence, and brokenness are as rampant in most of the body of Christ as they are in the world. Ravenhill's words regarding the condition of the world applies to the condition of the Church as well.

---

4   Katie Wiebe, "Christian Leader," *Christianity Today* 32, no. 15 (January 1987).

Truly the whole body of humanity is sick! To this terrible situation, politicians and philosophies of men have nothing to bring. The cause of the disease is spiritual. God and His Church alone have the answer.[5]

It is true that only God and His Church have the answer. Surely any member of any Bible believing Christian church would affirm that simple statement. God and His Church alone have the answer. But if that is true and Christians everywhere attest to its truth value, why do we look to the world rather than to God for answers to those ailments of religion? When conflict arises in the Church do we naturally run to the pages of the Scripture, to the altar of repentance, and to our brother whom we have offended to seek forgiveness? No. We do not. We run out the door, either to return to the world or to invade and then infect the trendy church down the street with our false religion.

God is not impressed with our new buildings because they house entertainment rather than worship. God is not pleased with our preaching because it bolsters the psyche and the emotions, but robs the listener of truth by using the Scriptures only as seasoning rather than substance. The Lord detests our incense and our many words not because of its aroma and sound, but because of its lack of sincerity. In many conservative Christian circles it is acceptable to rebuke worship paradigms that seem to be too entertainment driven. A hearty "amen" is likely the response to either the condemnation of the unbelieving world's unbelief or the modern Church's focus on numerical growth and entertainment.

Fellow conservative Christian, what about our legalistic devotion to the way things have always been? What about the preference on the part of *most* to maintain tradition rather than to nurture a drastic and constant heart-changing life-altering relationship with God which manifests in radical love for people? Where are the humble, gentle, and meek followers of Jesus that the New Testa-

---

5   Leonard Ravenhill, *Revival Praying* (Minneapolis: Bethany Fellowship Inc, 1962), 95.

ment declares time and again should populate the Church? Since when does demanding *my way* – albeit in "Jesus' name" – equate to spiritual maturity?

> When the world resists our fixing, we are inclined to blame it on the fact that it doesn't conform to our judgments, if only everyone thought like *we* think all would be well with the world. We feed our empty selves with the illusion that we are fixers rather than ones who need fixing.[6]

It is difficult to love God completely when our lack of love for His other creatures gets in the way. Religion has the inherent tendency of breeding a club mentality. We insist that we are the ones worshiping the right way and necessarily judge others who don't do it *our* way. Our incense is detestable in the nostrils of God because our worship lacks humility before God. The same incense chokes the world because of the judgment we cast over our shoulders while we are at the altar of supposed sacrifice, though it is secretly an altar of self adulation.

We worship our own preferences. We celebrate our own worth and ask God to bless us. When we worship our predilections we worship ourselves and it should be of no wonder why God's power has left the prayer meeting. In the first chapter of Isaiah, God expresses His disgust for the empty worship of the people of Israel. He even calls them rulers of Sodom and people of Gomorrah. The fascinating part about this is that apparently they were worshiping Him according to the mandates of their custom.

They weren't doing the wrong *things*. They were doing them, going through the religious motions, with the wrong *hearts*. Worshiping God with our lips and hands while our hearts are far from Him is the highest form of self deception and divine dishonesty. Who are we trying to fool? God! Surely we are not so foolish as to assume that we are able to deceive God. Who are we kidding then? One another? The world? Ourselves?

---

6   Gregory A. Boyd, *Repenting of Religion* (Grand Rapids: Baker Books, 2004), 137.

Jesus brings truth, not religion. The Church will never walk in the light of Christ until we are willing to rebel against dishonesty in all of its forms. The revelation of God is at war with our religion. We need more honesty and less piety. We need more repentance and less patting ourselves on the back for our holiness. The Lord has ill use of more religionists. He seeks worshipers.

> Yet a time is coming and has now come when the true worshipers will worship the Father in spirit and truth, for they are the kind of worshipers the Father seeks. God is spirit, and his worshipers must worship in spirit and in truth. — John 4:23-24

The Church must reclaim its prophetic heritage and seek purity. Not the purity of self-congratulatory praise, but the purity of broken worship which recognizes our own incredible need for God, out of which can flow honest and sincere worship. That kind of worship climate in the Church draws the people of God together because it tears down the walls of pride and opens the door for Kingdom life in a way that religion can only counterfeit and never create. The trouble is created when we are more concerned with institutional heritage of past victories than we are with the spiritual inheritance of repentant revival which celebrates the eye opening, illuminating revelation of the radical love of God in Jesus Christ.

His revelation is at war with *our* religion. The very institutions that we have created to get to God keep us from Him. The Church's adulterous love affair with its history has blinded it to the part of that history that pleased God and brought power into the Church – sincere, penitent, prayer-saturated revival. The question we must ask as we move forward is one of motives. God detested the incense of the Israelites not because of what they did, but how and why they did it. Speaking to the matter of spiritual motives in his classic work on prayer, George Buttrick writes the following:

> Prayer is a fundamental honesty, and therefore grants us knowledge of our motives... Christ is the "the brave Son of fact," and God conceived under the

image of Christ is realism... So real was Christ that Peter fell back from his presence with a cry, "Depart from me; for I am a sinful man, O Lord"; so real, that when he saw women weeping for him sentimentally as he trod the Via Dolorosa, he would not let them take refuge in any mere emotionalism: "Weep not for me, but weep for yourselves, and for your children." Christian prayer cannot easily be dishonest.[7]

Neither should Christian living easily be dishonest.

The bizarre disconnection between the radical life of the Church found in the book of Acts and the church found on the average street corner today is shelved on a far deeper level than that of programming paradigms and methods of Sunday school. It is rooted in motives and intentions. We fail to spread the message of the grace of God because we have not honestly conceived of the measure of the grace of God which has been poured out to us. We cheapen the Gospel with catchy slogans, slick campaigns, and easy believism because we have failed to taken an honest inventory of how deeply indebted to grace that we are constrained to be.[8]

I have a friend who I have known for many years who was stricken with cancer when he was a very young, healthy, and vibrant man. He was frightened and knew that there was a high likelihood that his life would be cut terribly short. When the alert doctor who found the cancer on what was only a routine checkup was also able to perform treatment and partner with surgeons to remove the cancer, my friend felt incredibly indebted to that doctor. He sincerely cherished the man for the help he had given him.

---

7   George A. Buttrick, *Prayer* (Nashville, Tennessee: Parthenon Press, 1942), 163.

8   I am here alluding to the familiar Christian hymn "Come Thou Fount of Every Blessing" which was penned in 1757 by pastor and hymnist Robert Robinson. The fourth stanza sings "O to grace how great a debtor daily I'm constrained to be! Let Thy goodness, like a fetter; bind my wandering heart to thee. Prone to wander, Lord, I feel it, prone to leave the God I love; here's my heart, O take and seal it, seal it for Thy courts above."

How quickly we forget the full measure of our indebtedness to God for His grace and prostitute ourselves with religion. When our sin and hopeless condition is weighed in the scales of justice, the grace of God should drive us away from man-made religious idols into the arms of grace because it is our only hope. Why, when we have received the tremendous flood of God's grace, do we so easily turn from its torrent and place our trust in the trickle of righteousness? How like blind men we stumble into the cesspool of our own religious undertakings for cleansing while the raging torrents of God's love scare us in the opposite direction!

The Church must regain its prophetic focus. This means individual Christians must repent of religion, pick up their cross, and follow Jesus. God is calling each one of us to bring to Him the sacrifice of a contrite heart and the offering of a transformed life.

> If we deliberately keep on sinning after we have received the knowledge of the truth, no sacrifice for sins is left, but only a fearful expectation of judgment and of raging fire that will consume the enemies of God. — Hebrews 10:26-27

Religion won't save us. In fact, if we are honest, we must concede that it always pushed people further away from God. Worship apart from actual sacrifice is vanity. Sacrifice apart from sincere worship isn't possible. Gomorrah was religious too. No doubt it had its idols and forms of false worship. God was neither pleased with them nor the Israelites who had the proper *form of religion,* but were as vile inwardly as Sodom and Gomorrah. What sacrifice is pleasing to God? An authentically repentant heart.

2

Spectators or Combatants?

> Do not suppose that I have come to bring peace to the earth. I did not come to bring peace, but a sword. For I have come to turn 'a man against his father, a daughter against her mother, a daughter-in-law against her mother-in-law—a man's enemies will be the members of his own household.' Anyone who loves his father or mother more than me is not worthy of me; anyone who loves his son or daughter more than me is not worthy of me; and anyone who does not take his cross and follow me is not worthy of me. Whoever finds his life will lose it, and whoever loses his life for my sake will find it. – Matthew 10:34-39

People's lives are broken. People's lives convulse and tremor in the darkness of ignorance of, and rebellion to, the Gospel of Jesus Christ. Meanwhile, the Church watches like spectators at a demolition derby. We sit comfortably in the stands. The only thing that we do with any regularity is, at most, provide commentary to the effect that "All of this is so unruly. Why would anybody participate in such madness?" The world perishes and we sit idly by, barely affected, full of excuses as to why we isolate and insulate ourselves from their need for Christ.

I remember a time playing flag football with a group of boys at the Somerset Junior High School in Modesto, California. One boy had decided to play both sides of the field by hiding a flag of the other team's color and then hanging both flags from the Velcro hitched belt from which dangled the flags. He did it largely in jest, as there was no way that he was going to fool anyone. The entertainingly cranky old Navy veteran who was our fill-in physical education teacher that day quickly removed him from the game and made him watch from the sidelines.

Not every member of the church is gifted or called to be the quarterback who calls the plays and guides the game. We are not all equipped with the strength required to break through the line for a close quarters block or to wreak havoc on the opposite team's runners by tackling them to the ground. However, the fact that we are all gifted differently does not shield us from getting into the game. The mere fact that we are gifted differently begs the question as to why we are not then using our unique gifts!

When I began to serve as pastor at my first solo charge in the pastorate, a man actually patted me on the back one day after the worship service and unreservedly said to me "Well, we finally got our new pastor and we are all looking forward to seeing how *you* build the church." These were his words exactly. My understanding of his sentiments were confirmed by the lack of help that he and the vast majority of other church members gave me in the work of the proclamation of the Gospel of Jesus Christ in that community.

This man was honestly ignorant of who it is that builds the Church. He apparently had no consideration of the fact that it is ultimately Jesus who builds His Church (Matthew 16:18). He had little recognition of the reality that Kingdom living is a joint effort among the people of God (Acts 2:17; Romans 12:4-5; I Corinthians 10:17; Ephesians 4:25). The pews of local churches are not supposed to be sideline bleachers from which to spectate while others put the Christian life upon display. Our Lord intends them to be the benches upon which sit the players who receive instruction, encouragement, challenge, and are equipped by their coach for the game at hand.

The Christian life happens in community. The notion of the Lone Ranger Christian sitting under a tree meditating on the beauty of God *rather* than attending the worship gathering of the local fellowship of saints is completely antithetical to the biblical portrayal of the Church that Jesus purchased with His own blood. Personal devotion is important but the Christian life is *necessarily* life in community. Eugene Peterson, in his book, *Christ Plays in Ten Thousand Places*, emphasizes the necessity of Christian community when he writes the following:

> The Holy Spirit is coming. This Holy Spirit will be in them, doing in them what Jesus did among them. … The way God was present to them in Jesus, God will be present to others in them … Everything Jesus said and did among them is to be continued in what they (we!) say and do.[9]

When we neglect the importance of Christian community, we neglect the very work of God in this world! What God is doing in this world He is doing through His Church. Our disunity with one another, our distrust for one another, and our disharmony in the work of building the Kingdom of God stains the beauty of the Gospel message. The Church is no longer the blood-stained community of the Cross. It is a sin-stained collection of individuals warring over personal preferences of selfish idolatries.

We fail to build the kingdom of God because we are too busy maintaining personal fiefdoms. I am reminded of the words of the old preacher who once told me that he had grown weary of wading through people's personal preferences. True religion is not comprised of social niceties, smiling at one another on Sunday morning, but holding contempt for the recipient of our despicably false smiles, behind which lie contempt in our hearts. The war for the souls of men rages all around us while the Church conducts infighting with trench warfare, fighting inner wars of attrition over

---

9   Eugene Peterson, *Christ Plays in Ten Thousand Places* (Grand Rapids: William B. Eerdmans Publishing Company, 2005), 236.

personal preferences when it has been designed to be a community of light and life.

Rather than uniting around the common and central aim of bringing glory and men to God, we bicker over which method of music to use to glorify Him and only as an afterthought consider how to be men of God. The common ailment in the local church is a willingness to accept and even promote a comfortable form of religion which is powerless to change the world through the transformation of lives. We no longer operate in the authority of Jesus Christ in the proclamation of truth and we no longer operate at the center of the grace which God has extended to us in Jesus Christ.

The Church is watching the world perish from the sidelines while the world is watching the Church for signs of life. We sit on the sidelines and we are not even united in that. We bicker from the sidelines and seek referees rather than pastors, moderators more than shepherds, who are willing to indulge our whims and unwilling to call the dead to life. Many pulpits are filled with funeral attendants, slowly eulogizing their congregations week after week, year after year, with niceties so shallow as to never tread too close to the truth that a Church which lacks the power of Christ lacks Christ.

Ravenhill says that "We have a cold Church in a cold world *because the preachers are cold*. Therefore, "Lord, send the fire!"[10] Lest we let ourselves off the hook too quickly, we must remember that the Church is not a group of people following the *pastor*. All believers everywhere have been called out of darkness into the light of Christ and all have subsequently been commissioned to be witnesses to the light. We witness to the light in community. Together. It is together that we will either put Christ upon display in unity and love, bound together in local fellowships which are essentially characterized by love, self-sacrifice, and service, or we will make of His saving grace a mockery, trading it in for a feeble self-indulgent religion. In II Timothy 3:1-5, the Bible speaks to this very matter in plain language:

---

10   Ravenhill, *Why Revival Tarries*, 113.

There will be terrible times in the last days. People will be lovers of themselves, lovers of money, boastful, proud, abusive, disobedient to their parents, ungrateful, unholy, without love, unforgiving, slanderous, without self-control, brutal, not lovers of the good, treacherous, rash, conceited, lovers of pleasure rather than lovers of God – having a form of godliness but denying its power. Have nothing to do with them.

The greatest tragedy of accepting and promoting this kind of religion is that it not only robs the world of Christ, but it robs the Church of the joy of knowing Christ. Practitioners of powerless religion are like men drinking from empty cups, cursing their thirst, but not hearing one another because their cursing voices are drowned out by the sound of the rushing torrent of a mighty stream only several feet away. Having a powerless religion is worse than having no religion at all because at least the pagan may be able to open his eyes to the beauty of Christ when he discovers it. The ears of the practitioner of powerless religion will not receive it because her ears are numb from standing so close to the river of life for so long and never tasted of its life-giving waters.

It is tragic that so many believers in our day have traded in the power of the Gospel for a form of religion of impotency. While it may save them from eternal damnation on the basis of the immensity of His grace, it will do nothing to save them from the destruction that overtakes them now. The propagation of social niceties and the proliferation of religious rules in place of the Gospel power, which is always displayed in transformed lives, presently populates the streets of Hell. Satan's greatest weapon is an impotent Church. There is a spiritual battle raging and we speak of our "*religious heritage.*" We sit on the sidelines in our easy chairs keeping up on the latest quasi-religious politically motivated debate while our neighbor perishes in his sin!

The well meaning religionist will surely offer rebuttal. "What would you have me do? Rush the streets like a madman proclaiming the end of the world?" Rush the street? Speak to strangers?

Fellow sloth. Co-worker in a powerless religion. Co-harvester of nothing in a field where the harvest is plenty. Have you and I gone to the room down the hall with the Gospel? How many Christian homes are *not* filled with casual and normal conversation of the glory of the Lord? How many Christian families have gone days and months and years *without* proclaiming His goodness? We bellyache and bemoan a popular culture that is devoid of the truth of Jesus while our lives are no less equally vacant of that truth, save for Sunday morning.

If we would see His glory manifest in society it must become central in the homes of His children! Then it must spill out into the local fellowship of believers. To put it as plainly as possible, we have got it backwards. The family is the institution of God's choosing for training children in the ways of the Lord. The Church empowers the family to train children in the ways of the Lord. It is not where we take our pagan children to become followers of Jesus. It is the place where followers of Jesus gather to encourage one another and worship the Lord.

The Christian family is the heart which sustains the life of the Christian Church.

> I believe God loves the principle of family. He chose family relationships as the dominant metaphor for New Testament Christians' relationship with Him and with one another. Christians become God's children (John 1:12; Romans 8:16; 1 John 3:2) – part of his household (Ephesians 2:19). Jesus came to, among other things, reveal God as Father (Luke 11:2; John 1:18; 16:25).[11]

Have we gone down the street to our extended family? Have we lived in such a way that we are on honest ground when we begin to proclaim Christ with our lips because we have long proclaimed Him with our actions? Do our friends and family perceive us to be religious busybodies or sincere followers of Jesus? I'm not

---

11   Steve Atkerson, *Ekklesia* (Atlanta, Georgia: NTRF, 2005), 135.

implying even for a moment that we can control the perceptions of others. However, God will hold us accountable for our actions that contributed to those perceptions.

From the springboard of our families we launch our children into the world to proclaim Christ with gladness through their love for Him. We go out into the world every morning and by our actions, demeanor, what we say, and what we do we either proclaim or slander Christ. I seldom preach a sermon twice. I prefer to seek the Lord in His Word each week. Up to now at least, there are only a few sermons that I have shared with any frequency. One of those sermons is called "Good News Shoes". I have a great pair of old brown leather shoes that I modified and only wear on the occasion of preaching that sermon. The rest of the time they sit quietly on a shelf in my study.

They are old slip-on leather shoes that I wore out before modifying them for this purpose. I painted crosses on the top of each shoe. I glued large rectangular multicolored buttons on them, each displaying a different day of the week. I painted Jesus on the bottom of one and Devil on the bottom of the other. They have "Jesus Fish" insignias painted on each side. When I deliver that sermon I remind people that wherever we go and whatever we are doing we are treading out a message. Some message. The question for believers is simply this: What shoes did you put on this morning?

Every day when we dress and leave our homes to go to our places of learning, work, or play we must decide – every day – what message will trod into the world today. What footprint will you leave in the dusty trails of life today? Will you leave the imprint of Jesus and stomp on the Devil? Or will you tread out the world's message all week and then seek absolution in one hour of religious drudgery on Sunday morning? This simple illustration may seem trite or cliché to some, but the broader implications apply to all. Every day we proclaim something. Why not proclaim Christ?

There is freedom in Christ. There is beauty in the love that He offers us freely. Surely God's desire is that His children, His family, walk in the freedom that He purchased for them at the Cross.

Christ did die for us. The Church's mission is about more than only reaching the lost. We are called to meet the spiritual needs of the Church. However, the edifying and evangelizing processes of the church are too closely linked and inherently connected to divorce one from the other. The Church has been fattened *enough* on the encouraging words of men bent only on winning the adoration of audiences. Our needs have been met and far exceeded. We know all too well how worthy *we* are. We know how much *we* deserve to be blessed.

The greatest need that the Church has in our day is our need to get down off of the pedestal of our life, turn our hearts daily toward Christ and walk in like manner to that which He walked this earth. There is a battle at hand and you and I have been drafted. We are not spectators. How wretched it must be for our Lord to have called so many spiritual disciples and ended up with so many parade watchers. How miserable is the spiritual condition of the Church that is called and equipped to shine the piercing light of Jesus into the looming darkness of this world, but has instead chosen to turn down the dimmer switch on the light so as not to offend the nocturnal creatures perishing in their sin.

We will never live in the center of the peace which God intends for us to have until we learn that Jesus didn't come to bring peace in this world's terms. He didn't come to secure national boundaries or to establish a peaceful and happy existence for His followers with no sacrifice. He is neither a political messiah nor a prosperity guru. The peace Jesus gives is hope in the face of adversity, eternal life in the face of death, and unshakable joy in the face of trials, calamity, and suffering. To be a part of the Kingdom of God is to necessarily adopt a different outlook on every area of life!

The Church lacks potency to the extent that it lacks a clear understanding of what it is. Jesus never played it safe. Jesus spoke words of life and truth and then went to the Cross to authenticate both. We are a part of the Kingdom that He came to establish. Are we really ready to take up our cross and apply the radical teaching of Jesus in our lives? Do we really believe that we should or can love our enemies? Have we committed ourselves initially and are we ready to commit ourselves every day to the radical nature of what it means to be a part of His Kingdom?

> The Kingdom demands *radical* decision. Some decisions are easily made and require little effort; but the decision for the Kingdom of God is often difficult and requires great energy of the will. Jesus said. "From the days of John the Baptist until now the kingdom of heaven works mightily, and men of violence take it by force" (Matt. 11:12)… The Kingdom demands a response so radical that it may be described in terms of violence and force.[12]

Christ has erupted into the world. The message of the Cross shatters commonly held beliefs about justice, love, and wrath. Jesus crashes into the world like a bomb exploding while the Church trickles like a single drop of water falling. Where is the power of Christ in His Church? Where is the violence of grace? What has happened to the *radical* Church that proclaimed and followed Jesus even if it meant carrying His cross daily and hanging on theirs in the end? Where is the radical love of God in a world so desperately in need of grace?

The peace which Christ brings is an inner and eternal peace no matter what we experience in this world that is fading away right in front of us. We seem to be under the mistaken impression that Jesus came to make peace *with* the world. While we are salt and light and love in this world, eternity is of primary concern. We are pilgrims, passing through. Jesus brings peace with God to sinners not with the world in spite of sin. Spectators sit peacefully on the sideline bleachers, but combatants are fully engaged in the battle at hand.

This world is not our home. This world is perishing! It is passing away.

> What I mean, brothers, is that the time is short.
> From now on those who have wives should live as if

---

12 George Eldon Ladd, *The Gospel of the Kingdom* (Grand Rapids, Michigan: Wm. B. Eerdmans Publishing Company, 1959), 99.

they had none; those who mourn, as if they did not; those who are happy, as if they were not; those who buy something, as if it were not theirs to keep; those who use the things of the world, as if not engrossed in them. For this world in its present form is passing away. – I Corinthians 7:29-31

Jesus did not come to bring peace to this world. He brings a sword. The Gospel often separates men and women, mother and father, sister and brother. For the believer, the Gospel is paramount. All of our affections radiate out from the epicenter of faith. I grew up in California so the analogous language of an earthquake is very familiar to me. When an earthquake strikes, it begins at one focus point where the tectonic plates have accumulated enough pressure and finally give way to a violent explosion of energy. That very spot where the quake begins is the epicenter. From there huge amounts of destructive force are thrust outward in waves of energy.

So it is with us. When love for Christ erupts in our hearts, waves of His love travel throughout our lives transforming every area of our life. His love brings destruction to sinful habits. His love crushes idolatrous worship of the many false gods in our lives. His love forces change in our lives because of the immensity of the power of it! His love is violent. His love rips our affections away from this world and places them squarely upon the worth and beauty of Christ.

Have you ever had to remove a small child's hand from something that was potentially or certainly destructive for that child? When you begin peeling the child's hands off of the item which, unbeknownst to him or her, will surely hurt them, they begin to scream, they fight against it. They don't understand. They think you are trying to cause them pain when in fact your *force* is intended to save them. The love of God in Christ is violent. God hates those things that come against His glory primarily because He is worthy and secondarily because they keep us from knowing Him.

You see, God is calling for the affection of our hearts. The Biblical message is clear that God desires intimacy with His creatures. He created us to know Him. The Lord is not impressed, pleased by, or interested in obligatory religious ritual. He wants our hearts. Salvation brings with it a radically different understanding of the world. The love that Christ gives is transformative. Commitment, religion's highest possible virtue, only regulates. Where love makes us want to do something, commitment, *religion*, only makes us have to do something. Religion says "check this box". Jesus says "Take up your Cross". That means that we are prepared to die. Carrying our Cross does not mean that we are patient with minor irritations. It has nothing to do with subtle religious duties.

What is your heart's greatest treasure? Are your goals for your life consistent with God's goals for your life? What drives you? Where are we getting life from? Is our affection primarily attached to this world or to Christ? When you or I genuinely love something, it consumes us. It may even become an obsession. When I first met Christina I was immediately interested in her. To tell you the truth I don't think the feeling was mutual. In fact, it has been well said that usually the cure for love at first sight is a second glance. When we started to see each other, she would play hard to get. As I began to fall in love with her, I would routinely give her flowers, teddy bears, and call her just to tell her how I felt about her.

Over the years I have grown only to love her more and more. After more than a decade together both of our lives are so interconnected that it is sometimes hard to tell where one of us ends and the other begins. Time and again the Bible uses the analogy of the Bride and Bridegroom to describe Christ's relationship to the Church and our individual lives are to be no less connected to Jesus. He is the lover of our souls! Following Him comes at a terribly high cost, but the reward for genuine obedience and love for God so far outweighs the cost as to discount it completely. He demands all of us and gives us Himself in return.

To the extent that we give all of ourselves, we will find the real peace that Christ brings. Salvation is not easy. Yes, it is very true that salvation is the gift of God's grace to all who will receive Christ by faith. Yes, in that sense, salvation is "easy." But it comes at a *high cost*. I was driving in the car just the other day with my six-year-old Sebastian and we were talking about having moved to Suffolk. He said "God told you to move here to be the pastor here right, Dad?" I said "Yes." He said "People always do what God tells them don't they?" I said, "Well son, a lot of people don't listen to God." His reply was "Ya, but everybody who loves God always does what He says." I tell you now as I told him then, even for those who love God, doing God's will is never easy. It is seldom the easiest thing to do, but it is always the right thing to do. It is always costly.

It changes everything in our life. Our priorities change, our affections change, how we spend our time and money changes. If it doesn't change then we may want to consider why not. Those who misunderstand the high cost of salvation often construct "magic formulas" or "golden calves" of various forms to cling to rather than clinging to Christ. For those who are unwilling to turn their hearts over to Jesus, it is often easier to trust in their baptism, their church membership, or perhaps their own goodness. However, the truth is that when we look at this world through the lens of the Gospel, we find that what we have found is not worth finding.

This world is not our home. We are pilgrims. Cling to Christ. Cast off the illusions of this world. Let go of the illusion of control which in our frailty we could never posses, the illusion of wealth which moths destroy and rust corrupts, the illusion of power which goes as easily as it comes, and the illusion that this world holds any worth that is in any way comparable to knowing God in Jesus Christ through the Spirit. "What is more, I consider everything a loss compared to the surpassing greatness of knowing Christ Jesus my Lord, for whose sake I have lost all things. I consider them rubbish, that I may gain Christ." (Philippians 3:8)

Are we spectators or combatants? The world perishes in its sin while we pat ourselves on the back for what fine religious folk we are. Lord, set the hearts of your Church ablaze!

3

Flunking Out

Before this faith came, we were held prisoners by the law, locked up until faith should be revealed. So the law was put in charge to lead us to Christ that we might be justified by faith. Now that faith has come, we are no longer under the supervision of the law. You are all sons of God through faith in Christ Jesus, for all of you who were baptized into Christ have clothed yourselves with Christ. There is neither Jew nor Greek, slave nor free, male nor female, for you are all one in Christ Jesus. If you belong to Christ, then you are Abraham's seed, and heirs according to the promise.
– Galatians 3:23-29

It has been well stated that God has no grandchildren. In the early days of the Congregational Churches in Puritan (Separatist) America, a matter in close connection to this statement arose. The Half-Way controversy arose over the matter of whether children of baptized but unconverted people should be allowed to be baptized as infants, as was the custom of these theologically reformed Congregationalists. In an answer to this question, the Half-Way Covenant was adopted as a solution by 17th-century New England Congregationalists, also called Puritans.

The Half-Way Covenant, as it came to be known,

allowed the children of baptized but unconverted church members to be baptized and thus become church members and have political rights. Early Congregationalists had become members of the church after they could report an experience of conversion. Their children were baptized as infants, but, before these children were admitted to full membership in the church and permitted to partake of the Lord's Supper, they were expected to also give evidence of a conversion experience. Many never reported a conversion experience but, as adults, were considered church members because they had been baptized, although they were not admitted to the Lord's Supper and were not allowed to vote or hold office.

Whether the children of these baptized but unconverted church members should be accepted for baptism became a matter of controversy. In 1657 a ministerial convention suggested that such children should be accepted for baptism and church membership, and in 1662 a synod of the churches accepted the practice, which in the 19th century came to be called the Half-Way Covenant. This step increased the diminishing minority of church members in the colonies, extended church discipline over more people, and encouraged a greater number to seek conversion and work for the benefit of the church.

Although this solution was accepted by the majority of the churches in New England, it was opposed by a vocal minority. The practice was abandoned by most churches in the 18th century when Jonathan Edwards and other leaders of the Great Awakening taught that church membership could be given only to convinced believers." Initially, many church members and pastors were in favor of the Half-Way Covenant. However, in time it proved to be a spiritual disaster. It greatly reduced the high view of the importance of personal conversion to Jesus Christ.[13]

---

13 *Encyclopedia Brittanica*, Online Edition, s.v. "Half-Way Covenant."

It reduced church membership to a legal matter, rather than a spiritual matter of the highest eternal significance. Instead of relying on outward evidence and personal testimony of conversion as a requirement for church membership, as evidence of the grace of God, the church chose a legalistic route. While the law of God is of supreme importance and teaches us of the holiness of God, it is inadequate to save. If a sinner is baptized, but fails to ever receive Christ by faith and profess it publicly in word and deed, that sinner is simply a *soggy sinner*.

Neither baptism, nor any other religious hoop that we may jump through or throw our kids through saves. Only Jesus Christ saves and He does so through personal faith in God who offers unending grace. The law is a schoolmaster to lead us to Christ. The law by itself is inadequate to save and any who come to Christ must come by faith, instructed not saved, by the law. Before we can personally know the salvation of God, we must know of our need for it. Too often today we instruct lost sinners in the beauty of God before giving them the key to even knowing God.

We have created a strange legalism where, in the name of only the love and grace of God, we enslave people to the law through ignorance of the law. In our deep desire never to speak of sin, we rob people of the means of accessing grace – *repentance*. By building our religion on the foundation of God's love for me because of my worth, rather than upon the foundation of the necessity of repentance because of my sin and His worth, we have stolen from sinners the message of true religion, which is a life of imitating Christ. But we cannot imitate Him who we do not know.

The Law is a poor substitute for faith. The Law of the Old Testament was a guide, a safe keeper, of the truth of God's character, nature, holiness, justice, mercy, love, and grace that would be fulfilled in Christ. As I have already alluded to, there are many ways to return to the Law. We can create a sort of legalism through never telling people of their need to repent of having broken the law. This dooms them to trust in their religious activity for salvation out of honest ignorance of the power of grace. Sadly, this is the place out of which much of the modern church operates.

Having never taken serious inventory of the depravity of their sin and the absolute holiness of the God they have offended, the modern day *love-only-legalist* is a legalist in the name of grace. Consider the woman who says, "Don't give me law and sin, just give me Jesus." In her ignorance she has precluded the possibility of knowing Jesus because He only comes to those who come to Him through repentance. "But unless you repent, you too will all perish" (Luke 13:3). Faith without repentance is like a tank of gas without a car. You have the fuel, but with the exception of decoration as a heavy load upon your back while you walk to your destination, it is useless.

The heavy load of the love-only-legalist, bound to the misery of religious works in the hope of earning salvation, will also greatly hinder and ultimately wholly impede her spiritual progress. There is a more obvious legalism which has also gripped many corners of the Church in our day. It is the legalism of the Judaizer and Pharisee. There are of course those who sprinkle in the grace of God in their Gospel understanding and proclamation the way one sparingly sprinkles salt out of fear of it causing high blood pressure. Legalism comes in many forms, but it is always at war with the revelation of God and always an ally to religion.

In Romans 3:20, the Apostle Paul writes:

> No one will be declared righteous in his sight by observing the law; rather, through the law we become conscious of sin.

In a subsequent chapter he says:

> The law was added so that the trespass might increase. But where sin increased, grace increased all the more, so that, just as sin reigned in death, so also grace might reign through righteousness to bring eternal life through Jesus Christ our Lord. — Romans 5:20-21

The Law highlights our need for grace. The Law teaches us that we can never do enough to satisfy the righteous justice of God which our sin has affronted.

What, then, was the purpose of the law? It was added because of transgressions until the Seed to whom the promise referred had come. The law was put into effect through angels by a mediator. — Galatians 3:19

In Matthew 5:17, Jesus says:

Do not think that I have come to abolish the Law or the Prophets; I have not come to abolish them but to fulfill them.

The Law always pointed to Christ! Speaking as early as Genesis 3:15 of the way that the Messiah would destroy the works of Satan, the Lord says:

"And I will put enmity between you and the woman, and between your offspring and hers; he will crush your head, and you will strike his heel."

The Law shows us our need for Christ. In a sense, the Church has graduated into the fullness of grace in Christ from the Law. When we make of our religious rules, regulations, and customs a means of modern Christianized legal bondage, it is as though we flunk out of God's school for sinners, rather than graduating in grace. In another more complete sense, the progressive process of God revealing Himself to humanity has culminated in grace.

God is the Lord of history. God maintains "that continued exercise of the divine energy whereby the Creator preserves all his creatures, is operative in all that comes to pass in the world, and directs all things to their appointed end." God's provision for the history of humanity is limitless. He extends control into all of the affairs of men as a sovereign Lord exercising absolute authority. However, within the boundaries of His sovereign decrees He has granted mankind a high degree of freedom in the exercising of their will.[14]

In the nation of Israel, God elevated humanity out of the barbarism of lawlessness and blessed humanity through Israel with

---

14 Louis Berkhof, *Systematic Theology* (Grand Rapids, Michigan: Eerdmans, 1941), 166.

the great gift of the Law. Many view the law only through the lens of its abuses in religious legalism. Consider though the condition of man prior to the Law. Rather than an eye for an eye, a person or tribe of people may avenge a wrongdoing through the destruction of a man's entire village and the taking of his life. The Law teaches justice. The Law of God puts the justice of God on display when it is applied in accordance with God's will.

There is nothing inherently wrong or destructive about the Law. Indeed, the Law is a great gift of God to humanity. On the other hand, the Law is not a means unto itself. It served and continues to serve a purpose of profound importance. It highlights our inability to meet the holy standard of God. It informs us of just how reprehensible our sin actually is. Many in the modern Church refer to sin as "less than the best for our lives." Wearing plaid pants with a striped shirt is less than the best for my life!

Sin is the breaking of the law of a perfectly holy and just Creator. Sin is high treason against the one who created and sustains our life. We will simply not have the ability to avoid the pitfall of either extremes of legalism that we have discussed here until we get a clear picture of the purpose of the Law and our relationship to it today. Above all else, the Law of God teaches us just how desperate our need is for the love of God. More than that, since the Law came to us as a part of the unfolding of God's story of love for us, it protects us from evil and guides us to grace.

Commenting on this passage, one commentator writes the following:

> It is unfortunate that the KJV refers to the law as a "schoolmaster" and that the NIV finds it necessary to work around the operative term by speaking of our being put under "charge" or "supervision" (v.25). The term [translated either schoolmaster in the KJV] is *paidagogos*, which means "a child-custodian" or a "child-attendant." The pedagogue was a slave employed by wealthy Greeks or Romans to have responsibility for one of the children of the family.[15]

The pedagogue had charge of the child from the age of 6 to 16 until that time when the child received the full rights of adulthood. The pedagogue was a guardian which protected the child while that child was being instructed until he graduated to adulthood. The Law was a guardian of the people of God which contained the seed of the truth of fullness of the grace of God until that truth was revealed in fullness in Jesus Christ. Writing in his classic work *The History of the Christian Church*, Philip Schaff states:

> As religion is the deepest and holiest concern of man, the entrance of the Christian religion into history is the most momentous of all events. It is the end of the old world and the beginning of the new. It was a great idea of Dionysius "the Little" to date our era from the birth of our Saviour. Jesus Christ, the God-Man, the prophet, priest, and king of mankind, is, in fact, the center and turning-point not only of chronology, but of all history, and the key to all its mysteries.[16]

We honor the justice of God when we live in the grace of God which was purchased at the Cross of Christ. Live in the fullness of Grace! Cut out the malignancy of legalism in all of its various forms. When we live legalistic religious lives, we dishonor the Law because that is not what it was intended for. We need to mature into a more complete understanding of God's grace if we are to avoid the pitfall of legalism in our churches, in our lives, and in our homes.

Is it any wonder the Church has so terrible a time retaining our young people? Consider the droves of children exiting the Church as they become adults. What have we done or not done which has left them with the impression that there is a time when one ages out of Church? Could it be that while they have got an "A" in their confirmation or baptism classes we have gotten an "F" in their spiritual formation? Kids drop out or flunk out of church when,

---

15   Boice, James Montgomery, *The Expositor's Commentary*, ed. Frank E. Gaebelein, (Grand Rapids, Michigan: Zondervan, 1976), 467.
16   *AGES Christian Library*, AGES Software Inc, Rio, Wisconsin, 2000.

rather than leading them to Christ, we only require their participation in our legalistic rituals.

Rather than planting the seed of the Gospel in children, we simply train them to jump through our religious hoops. We take a "Law mindset" to a work of grace. Religious instruction won't get the job done. Training a child in the way he should go has everything to do with pointing them to Jesus. He is the way. "Jesus answered, 'I am the way and the truth and the life. No one comes to the Father except through me'" (John 14:6). Neither religion nor entertainment will cut it; no matter how rigid and disciplined or fun and exciting it is. Instruction in religion is not what matters. Modeling and pointing children toward Christ is what matters most.

My heart breaks at how commonly I am told of, read about, or know personally churches warring within themselves, pastors at war with their churches, congregations abusing their pastors; all of which wars against the Gospel. How can a religiously idolatrous Church, more concerned with worship style than with worship not see the *destruction* that our religion wreaks on its practitioners and the image it gives in the world? We tell our children, "Don't be like the world," but the world not only offers more thrills, even in its duplicity it is often more honest.

In Proverbs 22:6, the Bible says that we are to "Train a child in the way he should go, and when he is old he will not turn from it." A parent's mandate from the Lord and our calling as the Church is to train children in the way that we should go. If it is common knowledge in business, corporate, or military leadership that genuine leaders lead from the front, why do we expect our children to apply lessons from our words, or more likely the words of an underpaid, under supported, and under appreciated youth pastor, that are inconsistent with what we put on display? Love for Christ is infectious to the modern generation that is starved for real love and reliable truth. Religion, on the other hand, is repulsive to a generation which has been trained by scandal and false fruits to distrust the liars and frauds that perpetrate them.

You or I may have a preference as to how best to train children and what their participation in the worship life of the Church ought to look like. I prefer that children do not interrupt my sermon or distract people from listening to it. One parent prefers that the children are in a Children's Church or nursery during the service so that they can focus on the Lord. Still another parent prefers to see children remain in the service because that is the way that they did it when they were a child. We all have preferences when it comes to the way that the Church trains children. Some of our preferences are rooted in valid concerns. No concern, however, outweighs our biblical mandate to train up children in the way that they should go so that when they are old they do not depart from it.

At the heart of that mission is what is in *our* hearts. Passing on religious tradition is not enough for today's generation of children. They are growing up in a vacuum of authenticity and intimacy. The family has been replaced by weekend visits. The community has been replaced by television and risks around every corner. They lack a foundation upon which to build their lives and we hand them a neatly wrapped religion, expecting it to deliver things that it is simply not able to give. Our children love what we love and we love the world. That is why our religion fails them and they toss it to the side on their quest for something more substantial. The world fails them, too and that is why they are disillusioned.

We need Christ in our hearts, not religion in our homes! It is not enough to bemoan the culture and weep for future generations. I sometimes tease my rambunctious sons when they make a mess of the car or the house by saying, "You better take care of this place. All of this is mine and I just let you use it!" They will usually sort of grin and say something to the effect of "No Dad, its all of ours. We're a family." In Psalm 127:3-5, the Bible says that "Sons are a heritage from the LORD, children a reward from him. Like arrows in the hands of a warrior are sons born in one's youth. Blessed is the man whose quiver is full of them. They will not be put to shame when they contend with their enemies in the gate."

If we care about the future, then we cannot model a Christian life which only consists of the fulfillment of religious duties. Tradition means a great deal less to a generation in which technology, global politics, the family, and every other part of life in the world has been revolutionized. Tradition matters far less to a generation fed the philosophy of pragmatism to the exclusion of moral values. If it works then it is good. If it doesn't work to your individual liking, toss it. To that generation the only thing that has the power to impact them for Christ is an infectious love for Christ.

The answer is not to be found in more light shows, high energy youth programs, or concerts. Those things may be useful tools and very enjoyable. The answer is not in Bible instruction, *catechesis*, or baptism alone. Engaging an entertaining, disciplined, even sometimes rigid, Bible instruction can be important. However, none of it will matter unless our training up of the next generation is driven by a desire to lead children not to the law, not to religion, but to the grace and mercy which comes in knowing Christ and knowing that we know Christ.

If the above statements about the lack of value of legalistic devotion to tradition and rules of religion seems in and of itself overly critical and too narrowly focused on the shortcomings of parents and churches, consider that children of believers stray because they *choose* to stray. What I am asking is what the preeminent underlying factor is as it relates to our present discussion. It is true that they leave because the world is more attractive to them. My point here is that often the world is more attractive because regardless of its problems, it comes across as more *genuine*. At least it is what it claims to be.

The church community has often failed to integrate them completely into the life of the Church. We are relying on a law mindset, overly focused on rites and customs. We must lead them to Jesus by our example, by connecting with them from the Scripture, and, if they stray, pray for them and love them. The trouble with many is that we are trying to win them to Christ as young adults after having missed a window into their souls as children. Parent, if you desire to lead your children to Christ, fall in love with Christ!

Church leader, if you long to make a difference in the lives of children, put the love of Jesus so obviously on display that the young people around you see it!

We have received grace, which calls us to a life higher than the Law. This is not a statement of detriment to the Law. This is the purpose for which the Law was instituted. God does not desire mere observance, but dedication of the heart. In fact, a plain reading of the New Testament highlights the reality that God has always desired a heart's devotion more than a head and hands obligation. We need far less religion and a great deal more participation in the love of God, less ceremonial boxes to check, more love *lived* out.

4

The Holy Spirit is not for Sale

> Then Peter and John placed their hands on them, and they received the Holy Spirit. When Simon saw that the Spirit was given at the laying on of the apostles' hands, he offered them money and said, "Give me also this ability so that everyone on whom I lay my hands may receive the Holy Spirit." Peter answered: "May your money perish with you, because you thought you could buy the gift of God with money!" – Acts 8:17-20

When my wife and I were first married, we lived in southwestern Arizona. For a while during that time, her mother lived in Mesa. We visited her regularly on the weekends and on one particular weekend we decided to visit a very large church that I had heard about from a friend. The name of the church is not important. It is just like hundreds, even thousands of other megalith bastions of American Christian pride, monuments to the gods of self and wealth, rather than the God of the Bible.

Upon entering the church building one is struck by the sheer size of the place. However, this is no ordinary cathedral. Its floors are covered by expensive marble. Its vaulted ceilings are adorned with ornate carvings and finely gilded details. At the center of the lobby is an immense foundation which aides the ambiance of wealth and prosperity. Just before the service was to start, the custom-fitted, silk-suited pastor and his richly dressed wife arrived in a chauffeured limousine. I was appalled at the superfluous nature of it all. After the service started, we were *treated* to a sermon about how to give to God in such a way that guarantees His favor in your finances.

Unknowingly, we had visited the house of the money changers (John 2:15) on the very day that a very prominent and well known prosperity preacher was visiting. After the service, I turned to my wife and expressed my absolute disgust at what we had just been witness to. Her response was chillingly accurate. "Churches have to do this because if it doesn't look like health, wealth, and prosperity is the consequence of attendance, most of those people won't go to church." She was right then and remains correct today. They have to maintain the *show* to keep the bucks rolling in.

There are a lot of people whose hearts are far from Christ, but live under the delusion of salvation because they have bought the lie of the prosperity preacher. They long for the gift that comes from God, but have no desire for the sacrificial life that is the consequence of knowing God. So many think that they are saved because they have prayed a one time sinner's prayer though their heart could not be further from Christ! The lie of the prosperity preacher is that salvation is like the ticket that gains one access to the clearing house of God's earthly material blessing.

God is not a slot machine. He does not guarantee that if we deposit ten dollars we will get back one hundred dollars. What a shameful mockery of the Gospel we make, when the focus of our sinful hearts is to get something more of this life from the very God who gives us the breath of life. How wretched and miserable is the state of the soul that cries out, not for forgiveness and the blessing of new life, but prefers conceitedly to remain in sin, mocking grace and providence, asking only for wealth and prosperity from the very hand that was wounded for the sake of love.

In Acts chapter eight, we see the magician of the ancient Roman world, Simon Magus, trying to purchase the Holy Spirit. He is rebuked strongly by the apostles. In fact, this is where the phrase "simony" comes from in the Church. That is, when some sort of ecclesiastical office or rite or spiritual blessing is bought or sold.

For our purposes here, we will not spend a lot of time dealing with the history of Simon Magus, though there is a great deal of literature and what some refer to as possible folklore about this man in antiquity, even in the writings of the Church Fathers. Suffice it to say that the spirit of simony remains alive and well in the form of the so-called prosperity Gospel, which is really no Gospel at all.

We often trade life in the Holy Spirit for a desire to purchase the power of God. Neither the Holy Spirit nor the blessing of God is available for purchase or resale. Give not to the Lord in order to receive a financial blessing. We cannot purchase the power of the Holy Spirit in any way. The Holy Spirit is the very presence of God dwelling within believers to enable them to live in ways that are consistent with the beauty of the sacrifice of Christ which secures salvation. The Holy Spirit is not a thing or a force that can be purchased. Life in the Spirit is the inheritance of God in Christ to every believer who has been washed in the blood of Christ – purchased at the highest cost.

Salvation is the greatest gift of God. When He blesses believers with financial prosperity it is not for the purpose of taking our lifestyle to the next level. He gives us prosperity so that we can reach out our hands and pull others out of the pit of poverty and despair. The Holy Spirit working in us means that He equips us to look like Jesus Christ to others, not so that we can get more of this world. The Christian life is not me plus Jesus, sprinkled into my life like extra seasoning. The Christian life is about dying to self, living for Christ, and being the seasoning of God's grace, mercy, and truth in this dead and dying world.

We need a clear picture of what the Holy Spirit's work in our lives looks like in biblical terms if we are to avoid the snare of the prosperity gospel. Its appeal is strong to Western hearts. While some believers have succumbed to it completely and even some unbelievers peddle it for the sake of profit in the name of Christ, much of the Western Church has fallen prey to it in more subtle ways. There is a great deal that could be said of the Holy Spirit. We could talk of the intricacies of the relationship between Father, Son, and Holy Spirit; the Trinity.

We could get sidetracked with a debate over speaking in tongues and whether such gifts are for today. We could do all of that and still leave empty handed when it comes to knowing what it is that the Holy Spirit does in the world and in us. The question which transcends all secondary questions and theologically nuanced conversations is the simple question that lies at the heart of living out the great calling of salvation in Christ: How do I grow in my *understanding* and *experience* of the Holy Spirit in my life? More specifically, how do I open my understanding to the reality that God desires to live His life in me so that the world can experience Him through my life?

That's why I want to focus on the general Scriptural motifs with regard to the Holy Spirit. That is, let's look broadly at what the Bible says about the Holy Spirit. Here are some of the general ways that the work of the Holy Spirit is accomplished.

In Zechariah 4:6, we see that the Holy Spirit is the arm of the power of God. "So he said to me, 'This is the word of the LORD to Zerubbabel: "Not by might nor by power, but by my Spirit," says the LORD Almighty.'" The real power in the universe is the arm of the Lord moving as the Holy Spirit sweeps, moves, crushes, lifts up, and empowers according to the sovereign will of God. At times the Holy Spirit moves and crushes armies, as in the Old Testament when God gave great military victories to the people of Israel though they were a small people, usually outnumbered and often outsized. The Holy Spirit is the power of God.

The power of the Holy Spirit doesn't always move in such dramatic ways. It has been well said that even a giant feels the sting of a bee. Sometimes God moves with great precision to accomplish His will. The key for our purposes here is that whether in dramatic fashion, as with the armies of Israel, or as the still small voice guiding our decision, moving us this way and that way, it is the Holy Spirit, the same one that presently dwells within me and within you, that is the arm of the power of Almighty God. The Holy Spirit is not something to be manipulated for personal gain. He is the power of God moving in the world and in you and me.

In Matthew 12:28, it is clear that the Holy Spirit destroys demonic strongholds. Responding to the claim of the Pharisees that Jesus cast out demons by the power of Satan, Jesus says "But if I drive out demons by the Spirit of God, then the kingdom of God has come upon you." Twelve step programs, for example, have the ability to help a man or woman bound in addiction see a way out, but only the Holy Spirit has the power to crush the bondage of addiction. While professional counseling has the ability to highlight our need for change, only the Holy Spirit transforms.

Dr. Phil can help point someone in a better direction in their life, but only the Holy Spirit can guide them into the will of God for their life. It seems fair to expect the unbelieving world to struggle in this sin-sickened, broken world, since they are striving in the limitations of self-power against the overwhelming power of the enemy. The world is in the world. People who are apart from Christ are like sailors lost at sea, without hope of spiritual power in this life and salvation for the life to come. Heartbreakingly, most believers are just the same way. The modern Christian are like throngs of young children thrilled to find a small broken piece of a seashell along the ocean's edge, remaining blissfully unaware of the vastness of an undiscovered ocean of mystery and bounty right in front them.

How like blind men are we as we wade in the ankle-high waters of self-empowered living while the depths of the ocean of the Holy Spirit-empowered life lies only a few feet beyond. The chief difference is that we are not without the power to dive more fully into the deeper mysteries of the power of God for our lives. Far be it for me to speak of you in vague terms about an indistinct mist of a Holy Ghost somewhere, out there, in some kind of mysterious spiritual fog. The Christian life which is lived devoid of intimate knowledge of the Holy Spirit is a vacuous Christian existence. While we do well not to over-spiritualize every vase that falls in our house or every ill wind that blows, what a tragedy it is that most of us only know of the distant story of another who is led by the Spirit, rather than knowing His leading ourselves.

In order to come into a growing relationship with the Holy Spirit and His leading in our lives, we must let go of the false idea that God's primary instrument of blessing is material wealth, physical health, and earthly prosperity. Perhaps the greatest gift that God will ever give to you or me is a life-threatening disease so that we can learn that this life is not primarily about this life. Maybe God's greatest blessing will be financial calamity so that He can teach us to depend upon Him through the heartache of losing this world and awaken us to the fullness of knowing His leading and peace no matter what the world brings along our journey through this life.

In John 15:26, we see that the Holy Spirit testifies of Christ. In John 16:8, we see that He convicts the world of sin. The Holy Spirit is calling men everywhere to come to the Cross of Christ, receive grace through honest repentance of sin and confession of the Lordship of Jesus Christ in the world and in their lives. The Holy Spirit draws men to repentant transformation, not to self glorification.

> The way of the Cross was once a gory road; now it is a glory road. Once the challenge was to take up the cross; now it is to ride a Cadillac and "rough" it smoothly. The offer to men is no longer the lordship of Christ in this life, but the promise of an all-expenses-paid, eternal honeymoon and a "mansion over the hilltop," with angel attendants and continual hi-fi music from an impeccable, million-voiced choir, world without end. How nice, but how unbiblical![17]

The way of Jesus is the way of suffering in this life in honor of Him who grants peace and beauty in the life to come. It is the bloody way of suffering, shame, sorrow, and death to self; abandonment to God's will. The Holy Spirit draws men and women to the Cross and then says, "Do likewise." In Romans 8:11, we see that it is the Holy Spirit who raises us sinners to new life. The Holy

---

17 Leonard Ravenhill, *Meat for Men* (Minneapolis, Minnesota: Bethany House Publishers, 1961), 116.

Spirit testifies of Jesus to the world and to believers. The Holy Spirit convicts the world of sin and draws repentant sinners, believers, into the fullness of life with God.

Christian, if you don't know and have never known the intimacy of fellowship with the Holy Spirit, how can you know, I mean really know, that you are saved? How can you know when you are in grievous error and sin? How can we experience new life in Christ apart from intimacy with the Holy Spirit when it is the Holy Spirit that brings that new life? The new life that we receive through faith in Christ is all about life in the Spirit. I'm not implying or even suggesting that life in the Spirit, knowledge of salvation, or conviction of sin is a feeling. Never mistake the Holy Spirit's presence for a feeling. Feelings, deep spiritual movements, moods, and sensitivities are among the ways that we learn to respond to the Holy Spirit in us, but life in the Spirit brings with it evidence of transformation.

The Church today is content to talk about life in the Spirit rather than live a life of redemptive spiritual value. We are more content to memorize Scripture than we are to live it out. We are far more comfortable praying for God to bless us than we are to ask God to use us. We have often neglected to teach about the Holy Spirit in evangelical Christian circles. In Romans 8:26, under the inspiration of this same Holy Spirit who dwells within each one of us, the Apostle Paul says that the Spirit helps us pray. Spiritual empowerment is the result of the Holy Spirit's presence within us. No believer can successfully navigate the treacherous roads of this life apart from the presence of God residing, empowering, living, guiding, from within.

In II Corinthians 3:6, we read that "He has made us competent as ministers of a new covenant – not of the letter but of the Spirit; for the letter kills, but the Spirit gives life." Commenting on this passage of Scripture, the late J. Vernon McGee of the *Through the Bible* radio broadcast says:

> "Not of the letter, but of the spirit." In the Old Testament, and specifically in the Law, the letter kills;

the letter of the Law actually condemns us. The Law says that you and I are guilty sinners. Those letters which were written on the tablets of stone condemned man. The Mosaic Law never gave life. That is the contrast he is making here. The letter kills. "For the letter killeth, but the spirit giveth life." I have often challenged congregations to name somebody who was saved by the Law. Did you know that even Moses, the law-giver, could not be saved by the Law? Do you know why not? He was a murderer! Also David broke the Law even though he was a man after God's own heart. Friend, you can't be saved by keeping the Law. The Law kills you; the Law condemns you.[18]

Religion leaves us doing it on our own, but the Holy Spirit, when He comes, brings life. Many Christians live as though they have been reading from the inverse- backward-translation of the Bible. In John 10:10, what is it that Jesus says? The thief comes to give, bring life, and build up; I have come that they may have death, bound in shackles of the law? No! Jesus says that our enemy, that is "The thief comes only to steal and kill and destroy; I have come that they may have life, and have it to the full."

The Greek word *perissos*, which is translated in this instance "to the full" or "abundantly," in some other translations of the Bible means superabundant in quantity or superior in quality. Jesus is saying that the abundance of God is excessive in nature. It is more than fullness of life. It is superabundance from God. In context of the life which Jesus lived and the life that He calls us to, it is superabundance of spiritual power not material wealth.

While we wade over here in the moderate waters of the shallows of "do it ourself" and "in our own strength," the Holy Spirit hovers nearby, our immediately available yet most often untapped resource for empowerment in this life. The question for today is whether our lives will become consumed by the Holy Spirit or if we will be consumed by the world around us. The question is: Will

---

18   E-Sword Bible Software 10.0.9, Rick Meyers, Franklin, Tennessee, 2011.

we grow in our dependence upon our excessive God or remain comfortable in a sometimes life of faith driven by a desire for God to give us a better version of this life?

I once heard a preacher tell the story of a very busy mother who went into her room one day at twilight to write a letter. She sat at her desk absorbed in filling page after page of notepaper. After some time she heard a sigh close at hand and turning her head, she saw her little son cuddled up in an armchair. "Why, Sonny, how long have you been there?" she asked. "All the time, Mamma," he said, "but you have been too busy to notice me." Ask God how long He has been with us, and He will say, "All the time." His presence undiscovered, because even the Christian people have been too busy to notice the fact – busy with their own affairs and losing sight of the presence of God.

We have been so busy doing it in our own strength that we have left Him undiscovered in the corner of our lives. We have tried to cut corners, buying into prosperity schemes of wicked and false preachers who suggest that the power of God is for sale like some kind of forever sharp set of steak knives at a flea market.

A significant part of the problem is that those same preachers and the congregations to whom they preach have succumb to the lie of the Devil that bigger is necessarily better and that the goal of every servant of God is to constantly increase his venue of ministry. The goal of ministry is faithfulness, not size. God is pleased with obedience not popularity. How many ministries have brought about more shame than good for the kingdom as a result of inflated egos and worldly living?

Writing in 1962, Leonard Ravenhill says:

> Just recently we heard Billy Graham in the Fair Grounds in Minneapolis thundering at the moral laxity of this day. He gave staggering statistics of illegitimate births and abortions amongst the teen-agers. As it was in the days of Noah, so also it is now. There was an ark then. Where is an ark of salvation right now? We need prophets for this day of doom. The light in the prayer tower should never be put out.[19]

51

It is not only the prosperity preacher that is to blame. While church leaders are largely responsible for the calamity of the indulgence in and exportation of the prosperity gospel in our land and abroad, believers must remain in the Word and in the power of the Holy Spirit rather than abiding in the teaching of wolves that scatter the sheep. Speaking of the Holy Spirit in I John 2:27, we are told: "As for you, the anointing you received from him remains in you, and you do not need anyone to teach you. But as his anointing teaches you about all things and as that anointing is real, not counterfeit – just as it has taught you, remain in him."

The prosperity gospel is not *the* Gospel. Jesus says come and die (Luke 9:23). The prosperity preacher says that Jesus is our celestial sugar daddy. Jesus says if you are not willing to die then you are not worthy to be my disciple (Matthew 10:38). The prosperity message is a trap of self worship. It is the false gospel message that God's primary concern in the universe is *my* happiness as opposed to *His* glory. Nothing in this world lasts (Matthew 6:19-20). The only lasting prosperity is in being known by the God of eternity who gives freely a gift of incomparable worth – life in the Holy Spirit through His Son.

---

19   Ravenhill, *Revival Praying*, 134.

5

Known by God

> We know that we all possess knowledge. Knowledge puffs up, but love builds up. The man who thinks he knows something does not yet know as he ought to know. But the man who loves God is known by God. – I Corinthians 8:1-3

A number of years ago I had an experience while working on my undergraduate degree in Biblical Studies that so shocked me that it has stayed with me. For the final exam in a systematic theology course, I understood the assignment to be to write a series of brief essays on several Christian doctrines. Well, I worked feverishly on the project. I really wanted to get a high grade since this class was a part of my major. When I submitted the paper, I was convinced that I had done a great job and I was sure to get an "A".

When I received back the graded paper a week or so later I was shocked! I had received a big bold "F" on the project. My heart sunk. I thought for sure there had been some kind of mistake. So I flipped to the back of the paper and there in big red letters were just four words, "Great job – Wrong test." I had misread the instructions and instead of writing a series of short essays I had chosen just one of the subjects from the list of ten and developed a full blown thesis! I had poured my heart into the writing, but I had come up short because while I had done a great job, I had taken the wrong test.

The professor was kind enough to let me redo the project and in the end I did get an "A". So the story does have a good ending. But I wonder how many of us, when we pass from this life to the next, will one day stand before our Lord and hear Him say, "Nice boat, great car, wonderful reputation, your knowledge far surpassed what was expected of you." Followed by the simple words ... "Great job. *Wrong test.*" The real test is love. The real test is obedience to God. The real test is not only what we say we believe about God, but how we actually do with that belief.

In Genesis 3:5, the Bible records the words of the serpent to Eve. "For God knows that when you eat of it your eyes will be opened, and you will be like God, knowing good and evil." Of course, humanity ate of the tree of the knowledge of good and evil and we have been judging ever since. Knowledge is not inherently evil, vile, or wicked. That is of course not at all what the Apostle Paul is saying in I Corinthians 8:1-3 and it was not the central problem in the Garden. The problem is that knowledge – when coupled with human frailty, imperfection, and sin – begets pride and judgment. It quickly becomes an idol unto itself.

The knowledge of good and evil drives our judgment of others as we constantly compare ourselves to others in order to prop ourselves up just a little bit higher than those around us. This is what religion is all about. Rather than living in and living out the kind of love that Jesus put on display during His time on this earth, we judge others, play church, and practice religion. Inauthentic religion, which is rooted in judgment of those who don't play by our religious rules, keeps us trapped from a life of authentic connection to God's love. It pushes the world further away from God's love because of our false advertising of what the love of God looks like.

> The fundamental problem behind the church's dysfunction as a bride and as a witness is that we have not adequately understood and internalized the Bible's teaching that the root of our separation from God is not merely evil as such, but it is the fruit of the Tree of the Knowledge of Good and Evil ... we are caught up

in trying to be the center; trying to fill our own emptiness, and thus trying to live by judging what is good and evil. We are thereby blocking the flow of love and thwarting God's purpose for creation and the church.[20]

We have knowledge of religious rules and practices, but the world needs reckless love. We have knowledge of religious heritage and customs while the people of the world continue to perish in their ignorance of God's love for them! Knowledge and accomplishments can be as destructive as ignorance and sloth. The greatest tragedy in the Christian Church today is comfort. The mantra of the modern Church is better programming to attract the world, but it is we who have been programmed by the world. The best use of knowledge is to cut the legs off of our pride. The more knowledge that we gain of this world, the more we see how desperately this world is crying out for a savior. The more questions that we answer, the more questions we learn are unanswered or unanswerable. The most learned must concede how truly little we know!

The greatest gift that God has given the Church in our day is a declining attendance roster and shallow treasure in the coffers. In order to be known by God we have to move beyond our own knowledge and judgment. More specifically, we should praise God for the gift of allowing a little pressure on the Church in our day in the hopes that it will purify the Church. Though not speaking to this specifically in its original context, the symbolic language is well applied in this instance. "His winnowing fork is in his hand to clear his threshing floor and to gather the wheat into his barn, but he will burn up the chaff with unquenchable fire" (Luke 3:17).

In the recent decades of relative comfort, political influence, broad social acceptance, and prosperity, the Church has become so comfortable in its religious practice that it has forgone the practice of imitating Christ. In the New Testament, discipleship is not a suggestion. Being a disciple of Jesus and having His teaching sweep into every area of our lives is *assumed* in the Bible. To be a

20   Boyd, *Repenting of Religion*, 104-05.

disciple is by definition to imitate one's master. "A new command I give you: Love one another. As I have loved you, so you must love one another. By this all men will know that you are my disciples, if you love one another" (John 13:34-35).

How did Jesus love? He did so completely, radically, and sacrificially. Those are the missing ingredients in the Church today. We don't love completely. We love God with our lips and deny Him with our actions. We love other Christians only so long as they love us. Our love for the Body of Christ is conditioned upon the extent to which we agree with them. Think this to be an overstatement? How many church splits can you name in your own community in recent history? How many churches do you know of whose growth is based primarily on transfers from other churches rather than from the making of new disciples?

Jesus commanded us to make disciples. That command was not to pastors, evangelists, or missionaries. It was to each Christian. What Jesus commands, empowers, and enables us to become is replicating disciples. If we are not replicating is it possible that it is because we are not truly disciples? Oh, we believe. Sure. We cover our bets by a formula sinner's prayer just in case Grandma's preacher knows what he's talking about. But do we become disciples? Have we moved beyond memorizing, quoting, and hearing the words of Jesus to living them out in honesty?

After spending eight years in the U.S. Marine Corps, I spent two years in the Army National Guard in Minnesota. I spent the first year as a full-time recruiter. The job of a recruiter is a lot like that of a salesman. In fact, all military recruiters receive professional sales training. There is another side to the recruiter's job. Just about every recruiter has served in a regular military unit of some kind prior to serving as a salesman for the military. He or she knows what it takes to be a productive member of a military unit. During a season of low enlistments, my office partner and I decided to take a different approach to what we had been using up to that point.

Rather than going about our task as salesmen, promising benefits and offering enlistment bonuses, we decided to act more like screeners. We would intentionally act as though we were only interested in determining if a person we were speaking to was *worthy* to be in *our* military. We were using a sort of reverse psychology and it really did work. We made certain that people knew what they were signing up for and, in raising the bar on the level of our screening, we saw that most candidates were more interested and more serious about what they were doing. We were no longer the caricature of a used car salesmen, making vague promises we could not keep. We were gatekeepers, ensuring the quality of the applicants.

For too long the Church has promised eternal life to the world while failing to mention that the condition for life with God in Christ is the death of the sinful man. Rather than appealing to the glory and honor of God and the high nature of the calling of being a disciple of Jesus, we have said anything, done anything necessary to fill the pews and keep the bank account in the black. To be a disciple of Jesus is to mimic love for the unlovely. It is to empty one's pockets to feed the poor. We are like the man who asks God to bless the fast that he takes by skipping his mid afternoon snack before stuffing himself at a buffet.

The Christian life is a radical transformation in the thinking, feeling, and doing in our lives. Salvation is the violent interruption in the sinful agendas of men. It is not a free ticket to an eternal paradise devoid of present cost. We don't earn salvation. But if our salvation has come at no cost, then our notion of salvation is at war with that of the Bible. That concept is foreign to the modern Church because for us the Bible is not a rock and a foundation. It is a source of support. It is a well spring of guidance to help us find the "real us." We have demonized truth and made a spiritual virtue of personal opinion to the detriment of our own souls and to the terrible disadvantage of the world for which Jesus died.

Admittedly, much of the responsibility rightly falls to preachers who are charged with properly and passionately expounding the precepts of God's word. This is true. As Ravenhill writes, "There is a famine of good preaching right now. The hungry sheep look up and are not fed."[21]   However, to what extent will the lazy, grumpy, selfish, idolatrous sheep blame the shepherd whom they themselves sought and procured solely on the basis that he is a master at non-offense? We have inverted the concept of the pastoral office, making the man of God a man who dare not offend the masses with "Thus saith the Lord."

The responsibility for the fatted waistline of the Church is equally shared by those who occupy the pulpit and those who occupy the pew. As Ravenhill writes:

> I am not sure we want another Pentecost, but we urgently need one! We pause here to get a refreshing and profitable view of the early Church as it is portrayed by J.B. Philips. As I remember it, he said that the Book of Acts describes the Church of Jesus Christ before it became fat and out of breath by prosperity, and muscle-bound by over-organization. This was the Church where people were not forced to sign articles of faith, instead they acted in faith. Here was the place where worshipers did not "say" prayers, they prayed in the Holy Ghost. His final slam is not less biting. These folks did not gather together a group of intellectuals to study psychosomatic medicine, they simply healed the sick!
>
> I am fully persuaded that this electrifying picture of the early Church is God's norm for his blood-bought Church in every age.[22]

The Kingdom of which believers have been brought into by the very blood of the Son of God is to be announced by the cries of bickering from within the walls of the meeting houses of local gatherings of believers rather than by the visible actions of imitators of Jesus. Consider the Biblical record in Romans chapter eight. It is specifically dealing with the question of whether or not to eat the meat that had been sacrificed to idols. There is appar-

---

21   Leonard Ravenhill, *Sodom Had No Bible* (Pensacola, Florida: Christian Life Books, 1971), 143.
22   Ibid, 19.

ently a division in the church at Corinth with regard to what is the right way to deal with this pressing issue. In the Roman world, it was common for meat that had been used in pagan ritual sacrifice to be consumed later in celebrations, even if it was just part of the animal, and what was left over to be sold in the market.

The question of whether a Christian should eat this meat raised broader questions. Should a Christian attend a feast where that meat was being eaten in part of a feast or a dinner? Should a Christian buy the meat in the market? If a Christian did eat the meat did it somehow corrupt them spiritually? We don't have to wrestle with such questions in our day, but this conversation does raise an immediately pressing concern for us today. When there are disagreements in the Church, how do we interact with one another? Within the Church, what is the ultimate deciding factor in the case of disagreements? Is it enough to be right? How do we treat one another?

Ultimately, Paul goes on to clarify that indeed food, whether sacrificed to pagan gods or not, neither defiles nor blesses anyone inherently. Food does not bring us near or repel us from God. What do we need to resolve problems in the Church and how do we relate to the world with all of its pagan customs? How do we deal with a brother or sister in Christ who believes differently from us – in this case about the meat sacrificed to idols – and when invited to eat the meat of the world sacrificed to idols, what do we do?

In the first verse of this section of Scripture, Paul says that "We know that we all possess *gnosis*, that is, knowledge." He is likely alluding to the high education of many of the Corinthians; they having been schooled in the knowledge of the great philosophers. He says "We all know that we have great knowledge. We are a wise people." But, "Knowledge puffs up, but love builds up" (I Corinthians 8:1). He is here speaking to the Corinthians who, through their use of superior knowledge, realized since the pagan gods really did not even exist, except in the form of stone or wood, that the meat sacrificed to them was fine to eat.

An imaginary god cannot defile food for a Christian who follows the only true God of creation. Speaking to these wise men, Paul is saying that while their knowledge is accurate, in their *gnosis*, they have neglected a higher knowledge. Remember, he is contrasting knowledge and love. Those who knew that the pagan gods were imaginary would eat the meat and have no reservation in doing so. But there were others in the church at Corinth. These were simpler souls, who had previously, prior to conversion to Christ, likely worshiped these false deities. For them, to eat the meat sacrificed to these false gods and idols troubled their conscience.

While those who ate the meat did so free of any burden to their conscience, they placed an unnecessary burden on their brothers and sisters who did not. When they argued with their brothers and sisters who refused to eat the meat, they allowed the matter to become a source of division and contention. It is not enough to stop short at having the right argument. The knowledge crowd was right while the scorned conscience crowd was allowing their past pagan roots to instruct their present Christian walk. While Paul does say that there were demonic influences behind these false pagan deities, trying to distract people from the worship of God, it was unnecessary to abstain from this meat.

It's not enough to win an argument. It is possible to win and still lose. We see this happening all across the Body of Christ. Churches are split and their witness to the unbelieving world is torn asunder as a consequence of right arguments. The situation in the Church at Corinth was very similar to that of today. There is an abundance of knowledge, a super explosion of access to that knowledge, and little know-how as how to apply that knowledge. We have access to all of the world's libraries of information through the click of a mouse, the pressing of a button on the screen, but we remain as unable to love, perhaps even more so, as we have ever been.

Knowledge without love is useless. D. L. Moody, the well known evangelist of the 1800's, once said that the Bible was not given to increase our knowledge, but to change our lives. Increasing knowledge of spiritual things does not equate to spiritual growth. Increasing love is the proper produce of spiritual knowledge. In Galatians 5:22, the Bible says that "… the fruit of the Spirit is love, joy, peace, patience, kindness, goodness, faithfulness." Knowledge of God and the things of God are important. In Proverbs 10:14, the writer records that "Wise men store up knowledge, but the mouth of a fool invites ruin." In Proverbs 1:7, the Scriptures recount the truth that "The fear of the LORD is the beginning of knowledge, but fools despise wisdom and discipline." The point that Paul is making is how do we apply knowledge. If we are right, but we treat our brother or sister in Christ unloving then we are wrong. It is possible, perhaps likely, to win an argument and yet lose.

Humility is love's first cousin. Knowledge apart from humility forgets how limited all human knowledge really is. We are His members, diverse in our make-up and performance, but duty-bound to blend our differences to produce harmonious music and praise that will attract the world instead of repelling it. The world tunes us out because we proclaim the transformative love of God against a backdrop of divisions and quarrels. God help us. What is it that Jesus said? By our knowledge and much learning the world will know that we are His disciples? No! By our love for one another!

We are filled with knowledge and opinions. We fight over internal preferences while God would prefer to see us serving the world. We will not see the glory of God return to His Church until we are filled with humility and honest, active love for one another. We will not see revival in our land until we find contentment in being known by God in love and grace rather than being content with our knowledge.

6

His Grace is Enough

Even if I should choose to boast, I would not be
a fool, because I would be speaking the truth. But I re-
frain, so no one will think more of me than is warran-
ted by what I do or say. To keep me from becoming
conceited because of these surpassingly great revela-
tions, there was given me a thorn in my flesh, a mes-
senger of Satan, to torment me. Three times I pleaded
with the Lord to take it away from me. But he said to
me, "My grace is sufficient for you, for my power is
made perfect in weakness." Therefore I will boast all
the more gladly about my weaknesses, so that Christ's
power may rest on me. That is why, for Christ's sake, I
delight in weaknesses, in insults, in hardships, in perse-
cutions, in difficulties. For when I am weak, then I am
strong. – II Corinthians 12:6-10

My little daughter Felicity, who at the time of this writing is a
bustling one-year-old, is a delight to our entire family, even though
she is on a near-constant treasure hunt throughout our home. Recently, she brought me one the spoils of her treasure hunting which
she had found in her older brother's bedroom. It was a sizable find,
a little plastic can full of tropical fruit-flavored gum. The lid on the
thing is difficult to open and requires a fair amount of strength. I
saw her struggling to open it and, though I would prefer she not

eat gum, I tried to open it so that I could break off a little bit of the gum to give to her as a reward for all of her labor.

At first she stubbornly refused to give me the gum. I explained to her, through my laughter, that I was trying to help her. She wouldn't budge. So I left the room and left her to figure out a way to get at her confectionery gold. A minute or two later Felicity came into the room where I was and brought me the gum. Apparently, she had discerned the error of her way and realized that she wasn't strong enough to open the tightly sealed lid. She realized her weakness and brought her problem to me. While I am always at least slightly reticent about comparing my relationship with my children to God's relationship with us, the analogy stands. In her weakness she was strong in my (albeit relative) strength.

> We will continue to live weak spiritual lives, devoid of the power of God, until we realize how much we are in need of God's strength. "It is truth in paradox that the more man becomes proud, the more he minimizes his own worth. The antidote? To gaze, not on man, but on God and God's providence." In other words, our strength is our greatest weakness. More specifically, our reliance on our own strength and our false belief that it is greater than it actually is keep us trapped in spiritual impotence.[23]

Only recently I heard a certain radio personality say to his audience, "Don't forget that we need to find something bigger than ourselves. Whether you find it in church, your family, or wherever else, find something bigger than yourself to believe in." Faith and belief have no power in and of themselves. Faith is an instrument which is only validated by the extent to which it is utilized to reach out to something worthy. Saying that belief in and of itself has the power to do anything good for the human condition is like saying that because I own a lawn mower I have a wonderfully well manicured lawn.

---

23 *Interpreter's Bible*, Matthew 10:30, page 372.

Perhaps the lawn mower is broken. Perhaps I don't know how to use it. Perhaps I am just too lazy to use it and as a consequence it has no effect on the condition of my lawn. Up to this point in the book we have been talking about the difference between false and true religion. We've looked at the enslavement that comes with false religion. When we are busy working to earn God's favor we get trapped in judgment, we sacrifice inner peace, we don't learn to live in the freedom that the Gospel brings, and we generally fail to find the fullness of the life in Christ available to us. On the other hand, when we learn to open up our eyes to the fullness of grace – He did it all for us, He sent His Son into the world for us, He called, saved, and is sanctifying us – we see the manifold power of God and His grace actively in our lives. His grace is sufficient for us in our weakness. Our strength is our greatest weakness.

In Psalm 8:2, the Bible says that "From the lips of children and infants you have ordained praise because of your enemies, to silence the foe and the avenger." This passage in the Psalms points to the reality that is fully unfolded in the life of Christ in the gospels. We are a part of an upside-down kingdom. In God's economy, it is not necessarily the most wealthy, successful, or influential people who receive or are given the task of expressing the worth and wealth of God. God chose Mary through which to bring His Son into the world. She was a poor girl from an obscure family in the obscure little Galilean village of Nazareth.

The Lord called the tiny nation of Israel through whom He would one day bring the Messiah. He used the elderly woman Sarah to give birth to Isaac and who actually laughed at the suggestion that she would give birth in her old age. Throughout the history of Israel, throughout the history of the Church, and throughout the personal history of you and me, God has been using the lesser things of this world to accomplish His aims and ends. The saints of God who are found in the pages of the Bible are no greater men or women than are you and me. In many cases they are far worse! They are sinners, adulterers, slanderers, murders, liars, and more.

God chooses whom He will based solely upon His will. Greatness in God's economy, prominence in the Kingdom of God has little to do with our ability and everything to with His glory and providential plan for the ages.

> But God chose the foolish things of the world
> to shame the wise; God chose the weak things of the
> world to shame the strong. He chose the lowly things
> of this world and the despised things – and the things
> that are not – to nullify the things that are, so that no
> one may boast before him. – I Corinthians 1:27-29

God chooses us based on His ability to glorify Himself through us, not our ability to make Him look good. There is a world of difference between the two ideas. God glorifies Himself in us to the extent that we recognize His worth, and as a consequence, we submit to His will and put His worth on display. This is not at all to imply that in the vile and base and lowest aspects of our human nature God is glorified. How base is the heart of the man or woman that bears the false witness of His glory through the proclamation of a life of sin. How dare we who are called according to His purpose excuse or dismiss sin in the name of God's abundant grace. That's a little bit like punching oneself in the face to display the glory of God's creation in having created us with the ability to heal. God is not glorified in our sin, our weakness, in that sense.

God is glorified in us as a result of allowing His grace to indwell and transform us and we will never be transformed until we recognize that transformation, as with salvation, is a work of God's grace. Just as we receive the gift of grace by faith, we grow in and His light grows in us as we submit to His will. Hudson Taylor, the 19th century pioneer missionary to China, once wrote the following:

> The awful character of sin is shown to mankind
> by its consequences. Man's heart is so darkened by the
> Fall, and by personal sinfulness, that otherwise he
> would regard sin as a very small matter. But when we
> think of all the pain that men and women have en-
> dured since the Creation, of all the miseries of which

this world has been witness, of all the sufferings of the animal creation, and of the eternal as well as temporal consequences of sin, we must see that that which has brought such a harvest of misery into the world is far more awful than sin-blinded men have thought it to be. The highest evidence, however, of the terrible character of sin is to be found at the Cross; that it needed such a sacrifice—the sacrifice of the Son of God—to bring in atonement and everlasting salvation, is surely the most convincing proof of its heinous character.[24]

In II Corinthians 13:4, the Apostle Paul writes: "For to be sure, he was crucified in weakness, yet he lives by God's power. Likewise, we are weak in him, yet by God's power we will live with him to serve you." Sin is reprehensible. It is an affront to God that required the violence of the Cross to make a way for you and me to be redeemed from it. Only through the brutality of the Cross could you and I be reconciled to God. God's justice had to be satisfied in order for sin to be atoned and He did that at the Cross. That's the point. All of the work that we do for God is simply in response to the Cross. Don't miss this! This is the key to this entire sermon series and the sum of true religion.

Our religious activity is the *consequence of*, not the burden *for*, freedom in Christ. That is a simple biblical truth but the actions of many in the Church today speak to the reality that many have simply overlooked it. Our neglect of sin and abandonment to the will of God is the consequence of grace working in us, not the burden for our work. Sin necessitated the Cross. According to God's grace working through our faith, we who were once dead in trespass and sin have been made alive in Christ. He saved us in spite of us, not because of us. He saved us this way precisely so that in our weakness, our sin, our inability, He would be glorified in us.

---

24   James Hudson Taylor, *Separation and Service or Thoughts on Numbers VI, VII*. Release Date: August 21, 2008 [EBook #26384], accessed online, http://www.gutenberg.org/files/26384/26384-h/26384-h.htm#page23.

He allowed the bankrupt condition of this world to come into existence through our sin so that in our brokenness He might bring glory to Himself through His Son. In our sinfulness, the blood of Christ covers us and His glory shines. In our inability we are drawn to a place of dependence upon God and His power shines in us. Speaking in Hebrews chapter 11 of the great lineup of saints in the Bible, the writer of Hebrews further expounds this Scriptural motif:

> Who through faith conquered kingdoms, administered justice, and gained what was promised; who shut the mouths of lions, quenched the fury of the flames, and escaped the edge of the sword; whose weakness was turned to strength; and who became powerful in battle and routed foreign armies.
> – Hebrews 11:33-34

Their weakness was turned to strength because they turned to the Lord. The same missionary to China, Hudson Taylor, that I cited earlier with regard to the nature of sin and the need for Cross, also wrote that "All God's giants have been weak men, who did great things for God because they reckoned on His being with them."[25] The same is true for all of God's servants, whether they are well known to the world or only well known to Him. Our strength is our greatest weakness. False religion which is built on working to please God, working to appear holy to the outside world, or any other false motive, is the greatest obstacle to knowing God.

On the other hand, when we are weak and humble enough to bring our weakness to God, then we are able to become strong in His power with His grace working in us, through us, putting His glory on display! This is a tall task, but it isn't our task. Becoming great in the Kingdom is about being about becoming weak, trust rather than control, submission over demands, sacrifice rather than gain. It is a tall task, but it is His task. We sweep up our broken-

---

25 Ibid.

ness and then bring it to Him as an offering and it is an offering that He will not reject. "The sacrifices of God are a broken spirit; a broken and contrite heart, O God, you will not despise" (Psalm 51:17).

His grace is enough because it is vast and deep and wide. We have it backwards in the Church today. We *venerate* the church sanctuary built by human hands while we *denigrate* the sanctity and the sufficiency of the sacrifice of Jesus Christ. We rely on our religion rather than His provision. The more modern local church is not less idolatrous in our day. In places where we have traded out stained glass for folding chairs, we elevate the *method* of ministry over the *purpose* of ministry. We rejoice over things that are not worthy of rejoicing.

We are more concerned with our idols and temples built to celebrate ourselves than we are with the grace and worth of God. Dear Christian, what are you joyous about? Do the bells of entertainment please you more than the chimes of grace? Are we more deeply satisfied and joyous in the beauty of religious life than in the beauty that was born of that shameful Cross? Is our joy actually a form of contentedness derived from pleasing ourselves rather than receiving from God? The old divine, Jonathan Edwards, said it this way:

> Another thing, that is often mixed with the experiences of true Christians, which is the worst mixture of all, is a degree of self-righteousness or spiritual pride. This is often mixed with the joys of Christians. Their joy is not purely the joy of faith, or a rejoicing in Christ Jesus, but is partly a rejoicing in themselves.[26]

His grace is sufficient. His strength is made perfect in our weakness. When will the Church learn that to lay hold of Christ in our weakness is the strongest thing to do? "Against the onslaught of iniquity, the race is not to the swift nor the battle to the strong.

---

26 Jonathan Edwards, *The Works of Jonathan Edwards*, ed. , (Peabody, Massachusetts: Hendrickson Publishers, 2007), 411.aq!w.

Here the lame take the prey and to those who have no might, He increases strength."[27]

To remain trapped in our self-elevated view of our feeble strength through dependence upon *our* religion is a strange thing to do in light of the sufficiency of *His* grace.

27   Ravenhill, *Revival God's Way*, 157.

Works Cited

AGES Christian Library, AGES Software Inc, Rio, Wisconsin, 2000.

Atkerson, Steve. *Ekklesia*. Atlanta, Georgia: NTRF, 2005.

Baker, David W. *Zondervan Illustrated Bible Backgrounds Commentary*. Edited by John H. Walton. Grand Rapids, Michigan: Zondervan, 2009.

Berkhof, Louis. *Systematic Theology*. Grand Rapids, Michigan: Eerdmans, 1941.

Boice, James Montgomery. *The Expositor's Commentary*. Edited by Frank E. Gaebelein. Grand Rapids, Michigan: Zondervan, 1976.

Boyd, Gregory A. *Repenting of Religion*. Grand Rapids: Baker Books, 2004.

Buttrick, George A. *Prayer*. Nashville, Tennessee: Parthenon Press, 1942.

Edwards, Jonathan. *The Works of Jonathan Edwards*. Edited by . Peabody, Massachusetts: Hendrickson Publishers, 2007.

E-Sword Bible Software 10.0.9. Rick Meyers, Franklin, Tennessee, 2011.

Ladd, George Eldon. *The Gospel of the Kingdom*. Grand Rapids, Michigan: Wm. B. Eerdmans Publishing Company, 1959.

Manton, Thomas. *The Complete Works of Thomas Manton*. Edited by Thomas Smith. London: James Nisbet & Company, 1871.

Peterson, Eugene. *Christ Plays in Ten Thousand Places*. Grand Rapids: William B. Eerdmans Publishing Company, 2005.

QuickVerse Platinum (14.0.2.1). Findex.com Inc, Omaha, NE, 2010.

Ravenhill, Leonard. *Meat For Men*. Minneapolis, Minnesota: Bethany House Publishers, 1961.

Ravenhill, Leonard. *Revival Praying*. Minneapolis: Bethany Fellowship Inc, 1962.

Ravenhill, Leonard. *Sodom Had No Bible*. Pensacola, Florida: Christian Life Books, 1971.

Ravenhill, Leonard. *Why Revival Tarries*. Minneapolis, Minnesota: Bethany House Publishers, 1986.

Taylor, James Hudson, Separation and Service or Thoughts on Numbers VI, VII. Release Date: August 21, 2008 [EBook #26384], accessed online, http://www.gutenberg.org/files/26384/26384-h/26384-h.htm#page23.

Wiebe, Katie. "Christian Leader." *Christianity Today* 32, no. 15 (January 1987).

Also by Chris Surber

Sweet Potatoes in My Coffee is an inspirational book based on a series of sermons delivered at First Congregational Church by Chris Surber entitled "Living The Grace Filled Life!" The book's title comes from an incident involving the author, his then 15 month old son, some coffee, and some Sweet Potatoes! The grace-filled life is about relating rightly to God as loving Father, relating rightly to one another out of a desire to participate in God's love and grace, and seeing oneself as God sees us; forgiven and free!
Available on Amazon.com.

The Sacred Journey is not a long book, and could easily be read as an eight day devotional for individuals, or an eight week discussion base for groups. It is definitely designed to encourage and exhort the church—one member at a time. – FaithWriters

More from Energion Publications

Personal Study

Finding My Way in Christianity	Herold Weiss	$16.99
Holy Smoke! Unholy Fire	Bob McKibben	$14.99
The Jesus Paradigm	David Alan Black	$17.99
When People Speak for God	Henry Neufeld	$17.99
The Sacred Journey	Chris Surber	$11.99

Christian Living

Faith in the Public Square	Robert D. Cornwall	
Grief: Finding the Candle of Light	Jody Neufeld	$8.99
I Want to Pray	Perry M. Dalton	$7.99
Soup Kitchen for the Soul	Renee Crosby	$12.99
Crossing the Street	Robert LaRochelle	$16.99

Bible Study

Learning and Living Scripture	Lentz/Neufeld	$12.99
From Inspiration to Understanding	Edward W. H. Vick	$24.99
Luke: A Participatory Study Guide	Geoffrey Lentz	$8.99
Philippians: A Participatory Study Guide	Bruce Epperly	$9.99
Ephesians: A Participatory Study Guide	Robert D. Cornwall	$9.99

Theology

The Politics of Witness	Allan R. Bevere	$9.99
Ultimate Allegiance	Robert D. Cornwall	$9.99
History and Christian Faith	Edward W. H. Vick	$9.99
The Adventists' Dilemma	Edward W. H. Vick	$14.99
The Church Under the Cross	William Powell Tuck	$11.99

Ministry

Clergy Table Talk	Kent Ira Groff	$9.99
Out of This World	Darren McClellan	$24.99

Generous Quantity Discounts Available

Dealer Inquiries Welcome

Energion Publications — P.O. Box 841

Gonzalez, FL_ 32560

Website: http://energionpubs.com

Phone: (850) 525-3916

www.ingramcontent.com/pod-product-compliance
Lightning Source LLC
Chambersburg PA
CBHW031606040426
42452CB00006B/421